Praise for *The Yoga of Cleaning*

Finally, this is a book that elevates home cleaning to a whole new level. Jen's perspective on how caring for and organizing a home does for our surroundings what yoga does for our minds, bodies and souls is brilliant! She teaches us to approach cleaning not as a never-ending chore, but as a means to restore order and serenity to our environment and to embrace the process. This book is an easy, no-fuss guide to making your home a sanctuary.

Carolyn Forte
Director Home Appliances and Cleaning Products
Good Housekeeping Research Institute

In the yoga world, a popular meme is to take the practice off the mat and bring it into daily life. **The Yoga of Cleaning** does just that in full force and with playful intention. This very fascinating book poses the surprising interplay between yogic principles, yogic philosophy and the processes of cleaning. **The Yoga of Cleaning** is not just an esoteric overview that attempts to stimulate a deeper awareness and sense of spirituality to cleaning. Nor is it simply a "how to" cleaning manual. Instead, Avgerinos has produced a work that merges the two in an engaging fashion, introducing the reader to methods that inspire otherwise mundane household and personal chores to something of a higher purpose. She reminds us that all actions have meaning and impact on our lives. She supports the process with holistic, efficient and streamlined strategies for care of the self and its surroundings.

Steven Weiss, MS, DC, RYT - author of
The Injury-Free Yoga Practice

When the routine task of cleaning becomes a spiritual practice, a new sense of order and calm enters your life. Let The Yoga of Cleaning *be your guide.*

Christiane Northrup, M.D., ob/gyn physician and
ne New York Times bestsellers: *Women's Bodies,*
Women's Wisdom and The Wisdom of Menopause

The
Yoga
of
Cleaning

An Essential Guide

SPIRITUALIZE YOUR CLEANING ROUTINE
AND
CREATE SACRED SPACE

Jennifer Carter Avgerinos

BALBOA
PRESS

A DIVISION OF HAY HOUSE

Balboa Press books may be ordered through booksellers or by contacting:

Balboa Press
A Division of Hay House
1663 Liberty Drive
Bloomington, IN 47403
www.balboapress.com
1 (877) 407-4847

Because of the dynamic nature of the Internet, any web addresses or links contained in this book may have changed since publication and may no longer be valid. The views expressed in this work are solely those of the author and do not necessarily reflect the views of the publisher, and the publisher hereby disclaims any responsibility for them.

The author of this book does not dispense medical advice or prescribe the use of any technique as a form of treatment for physical, emotional, or medical problems without the advice of a physician, either directly or indirectly. The intent of the author is only to offer information of a general nature to help you in your quest for emotional and spiritual well-being. In the event you use any of the information in this book for yourself, which is your constitutional right, the author and the publisher assume no responsibility for your actions.

Any people depicted in stock imagery provided by Shutterstock are models,
and such images are being used for illustrative purposes only.
Certain stock imagery © Shutterstock.

ISBN: 978-1-4525-9270-1 (sc)
ISBN: 978-1-4525-9271-8 (e)

Library of Congress Control Number: 2014902976

Printed in the United States of America.

Balboa Press rev. date: 02/24/2014

For HB

Contents

Introduction

What is *The Yoga of Cleaning*? These are two activities that don't usually go together. Or do they? Yoga means union or yoking of the mind, body and spirit. When these three aspects of us are brought to the task of cleaning (which is the art of purification) a greater expansion of well-being is created. When cleaning is combined with the technologies of yoga and its sister philosophies - ayurveda, meditation and vastu, the result is the cultivation of sacred space within our homes and within our lives.

According to a June 2013 consumer study, the idea that a clean home can help protect the family's health is well established, as 9 in 10 consumers surveyed somewhat or strongly agree that maintaining a clean home is a good way to stay healthy. Other studies have shown that a neat, clean and organized home can actually lower cortisol levels (in women anyway). There is a clear connection between cleaning and well-being.

You do not need to practice yoga to read this book and you need not be a germ-a-phobe either. This essential guide is the unique result of my own personal journey as a student and teacher of yoga and as a professional in the world of consumer cleaning tools, along with some AH HA moments that I have gained along the way. As a certified yoga teacher, I desire natural, healthy solutions for my own life and for the world. As a Senior Brand Marketing Manager for a global cleaning tools company, it has been my job to know and understand the world of home cleaning and the impact that it has on our lives. Although there exist many books on yoga and many books on cleaning, this is the first to unite yoga (well-being) and cleaning because they should no longer be considered mutually exclusive.

For starters, we need to understand that everything is connected. Living a healthy life doesn't stop with exercising on a regular basis and getting the right diet. We need to stop bombing our homes with chemicals that degrade our health. We need to stop letting our stuff own us, and we need to find a little mental space somewhere in our very busy lives to just breathe.

We need to care for our bodies as we care for our homes, and care for our homes as we care for our bodies. We need to create a little bit of sanctuary in our lives and that starts at home. It is very difficult to cultivate inner peace if our surroundings are chaotic, cluttered, or full of toxic fumes that can make us sick. This book is for anyone who wants to claim their life (mind, body and spirit) and their space.

Also, it might be helpful to understand how each room in your house relates to your body in an energetic (chakra) way. When you clean the kitchen for instance, you are connecting, clearing and opening energetic blocks to your heart center. Cleaning the bathroom will help you open your solar plexus center, and so on. Often people who have issues with clutter tend to be blocked in much of their energy body. We will explore the connection that cleaning has on well-being on a yogic level.

Cleaning is an everyday task that few of us can avoid. This is the perfect opportunity to practice karma yoga or selfless service - the desire to serve the divine in everything and become one with everything (yes, even the toilet). *The Yoga of Cleaning* is an invitation to spiritualize your cleaning routine and create sacred space in your home versus merely performing mundane tasks in a way that serves no one. This can be done by giving your cleaning tasks your full attention and staying present in the moment - becoming one with everything that you focus your awareness on.

Or perhaps you prefer to practice bhakti yoga or pure love and devotion. This could be done by chanting a mantra, repeating an affirmation, sending love and light to someone in particular or the world in general all while you are performing routine cleaning tasks. This new way of viewing our chores brings a higher vibration to us and to everything that we do.

How To Use This Book

This book is a guide through the essentials of yoga and its sister philosophies and how we can use them off the mat and inside our homes, especially when cleaning and creating sacred space. These are ancient concepts that were founded long ago in India - yoga, breathing, meditation, ayurveda and vastu. Ayurveda is a science of life that gives us guidance on balancing our unique mind/body constitution with our environment and vastu is the science of space planning that predates feng shui. These ancient techniques are still so relevant and practical today. Many of these subjects are too vast to cover in their entirety, but this book will get you started with the essentials. I will provide other references that I have found useful so that you can go deeper into any of these concepts. I will also guide you through the essentials of decluttering and natural effective cleaning. I have tested out all of the natural cleaning recipes in this book and use many of them in my own life.

You are your own best teacher. Take the tools and information that work for you based on your lifestyle and intuition. Integrate the technologies into your life that make sense and leave the ones that don't for now. The idea here is to move in the direction of something that makes your life easier, less stressful and more nurturing. Small changes over time can add up to big improvements. It doesn't have to be all or nothing.

I will not overwhelm you with the ancient language of yoga called Sanskrit except for a few indispensable words like pose and breath names. When I use Sanskrit I will also provide the English translation. I will provide a glossary at the end of the book that defines all of the Sanskrit words used. Readers looking for more information on teachers, systems and other resources can find that in the appendix, *Sources of Further Information*. I have incorporated infographics, drawings and photos that visually represent the concepts that I am trying to share. I hope that you find this book useful. Enjoy!

1 Journey Into The Yoga of Cleaning

*I was in yoga the other day. I was in full lotus position. My chakras
were all aligned. My mind is cleared of all clutter and I'm looking
out of my third eye and everything that I'm supposed to be
doing. It's amazing what comes up, when you sit in that silence.
Mama keeps whites bright like the sunlight,
Mama's got the magic of Clorox.*
~ Ellen DeGeneres

My Journey

It was in 2010 that I took the leap from a more passive interest in yoga, to an intensive study of this technology as I pursued my yoga teacher certification at the Internationally known Chopra Center in Carlsbad, California. Having read most of Deepak Chopra's books, and having watched him on the Oprah Show since I was in high school, I was drawn to going further on my path toward enlightenment because of his teachings.

It turned out to be one of the most profound experiences of my life and a journey that I will never forget. It took me a year to complete the training and get certified and I had to fly across the country from Connecticut to California four times in the process. Along the way I met some amazing people and most of all got to know myself at a much deeper level, learning techniques that would impact all of the other areas of my life including my professional work, my relationships and the way I respond to the world outside of me in every moment. This applies most to the everyday mundane tasks - the areas of our lives that offer the best opportunity to release resistance and live in present moment awareness.

When I began this journey, I was like so many others out there - stressed, busy, trying to find meaning in my life and a few moments of peace and calmness. I wanted to manifest my dreams and be my best possible self. I, like so many other women, was driven to be successful in all areas of my life. My then 10 year yoga practice offered me space, flexibility and peace but only when I was actually on the matt, and inside of a class. The other areas of my life were hectic, stressful and cluttered. As soon as I returned to daily life and work, the stress returned. I was looking for something that would offer me some relief and peace in a more lasting way. I had by this time read literally hundreds of self help books - books on spirituality, healing, and the metaphysical. I had read books on manifestation, allowing, meditation, intention and inspiration. I had read books on yoga, yoga philosophy, energy healing and crystals. I stopped listening to or reading the news outside of my industry, and only surrounded myself with positive, life affirming information. I became a vegetarian. Even thought it scared me, I cleared out some old relationships that no longer served me. I started a meditation practice. I connected with nature and I started journaling. I made a plan to clean up old debt and I am still working on that with the help of my beloved husband. I surrendered to the unknown, and took a leap of faith. Things slowly started to shift.

The lessons that I was learning were way outside of what I grew up with. I was born into a rather conservative and religious southern family. Raised by my mother and grandmother, they did the best they could, but the Eastern based techniques and practices that I was cultivating were a huge departure from everything I knew up to that point.

The changes that I wanted to make did not happen overnight. Things were still very dualistic for me. I felt calm, centered and loving when I was reading, in yoga classes or going through my training in retreat with other people like me, but then stressed and frustrated in other areas of my life. I was still very reactive in certain situations. Calm on the outside but fiery on the inside, I had not yet learned how to integrate the pieces and I did not have the luxury of dropping out and going on retreat fulltime. I couldn't just meditate all day. I had stuff to do, places to go and bills to pay. I had responsibilities.

As I went deeper into my yoga training and firmly developed my meditation practice during a weeklong retreat at the Chopra Center called Seduction of Spirit - that's when things really started to shift. On the outside people perceived me as calm and capable. They had no way of knowing the kind of monkey chatter that went on in my head 24/7. But after coming back from this retreat, people started noticing an outward change in me. I was starting to make peace with my spirit. People told me that I seemed more confident and peaceful, and I was. I felt more harmonious because I was connecting with my higher self. The techniques that I learned were really helping me to understand myself and what I needed in order to live a healthy and balanced life.

This may seem dramatic, but it felt as if the teachings of yoga were saving my life. Without it, I think that stress and anxiety would have overwhelmed me and made me seriously ill. I had a limited support group around me. My family, who has lived far away for most of my adult life and my friends were busy with their own lives. It was up to me to take care of my own well-being.

Although this journey is ongoing, I have now learned to integrate both sides of my life more seamlessly. I think that teaching yoga to both kids and adults has had a huge impact on me, both personally and professionally. Teach, so that you can learn. I have learned to incorporate breathing, mantra, ayurveda and other techniques that we will discuss in this book, into my work, life and home. This is why yoga has become so popular in recent years. People are starting to discover the obvious and immediate benefits that it provides. This stuff really works!

During this time as I was discovering my dharma or true purpose in life, I was also a Brand Manager for a global cleaning tools company located in Connecticut. We sold cleaning tools to major retailers in the home center, hardware, grocery and specialty channels worldwide. I sat in focus groups and listen to women talk about cleaning and what they liked and didn't like about it - how important and centric it was to their lives and their family's lives. I looked at report after report from third party sources for consumer insights into cleaning. I looked at tons of data on what people were buying, what their biggest challenges were and stats and studies on everything from indoor air pollution to natural cleaning and aromatherapy for cancer survivors. I visited store after store and trade show after trade show. The more research that I saw and the more people that I talked to, the more it became clear that there was a link between my yoga training and all of the knowledge and insight that I was gaining about cleaning in my professional life. My yoga lifestyle was creeping into the way that I viewed the task of cleaning, and it became clear to me that it was really just an extension of being healthy and living a clean life (no pun intended). It began to dawn on me that the universe had put me in that job for a reason.

When I stopped using caustic floor cleaning chemicals at home and used microfiber and water instead, my allergies got better. When I stopped using household air fresheners and used essential oils instead, I felt more refreshed and the house smelled better. When I made folding laundry a meditation instead of seeing it as a chore, I felt more relaxed and less anxious.

It was when I was asked to speak at a public relations event for a newly launched brand from the perspective of a yoga teacher and a cleaning expert that my two seemingly separate worlds fused into one, and the idea for this book was born. All of the hard research on consumer insights, the benefits of natural cleaning, scented dusting and the effects of clutter on stress levels came together with what I knew intuitively as a yoga teacher. At that moment, it became clear to me that cleaning can have a great effect on our well-being and that these two subjects are intrinsically connected.

The pathways of yoga and cleaning have shaped my life and offered me gifts that I never could have imagined. I have been able to create sacred space for myself within my life using the tools contained within this book. I have also had the pleasure and experience of helping to shape the lives of many students over the years.

Perhaps you are considering the world of yoga and holistic lifestyle for the first time and this book will serve as an introduction to a new way of thinking and living. Keep an open mind as you read this book. Yoga and natural cleaning can change your life like it has changed mine. I am offering useful information that you can integrate everyday into your home - on and off the yoga mat and outside of the yoga studio. Perhaps you will be inspired to delve deeper into some of the subjects contained within this book such as ayurveda or vastu. These are huge subjects unto themselves that can be studied for a lifetime. I encourage you take a leap of faith and start your own journey and revolution, discovering a healthier and more passionate life. There is little to loose and much to gain. As we explore each topic, I will introduce you to other teachers and books that have inspired me along my path. So let's get started.

2 An Introduction To Yoga

A Yoga motto: Don't just do something - sit there!

Why is yoga so popular right now? In my opinion, it is because people are hungry for direct spiritual experience. Whether you seek enlightenment, physical fitness, a mental challenge, or a way to relax, chances are there is a form of yoga tailored just for you. One of the most beautiful things about yoga is its inherent flexibility. Yoga is big and diverse, and can be adapted to you and your needs. In the last 50 years or so as yoga has spread around the globe, it has been interpreted and remixed so that everyone can derive a little something from the ancient ways. It can be devotional/ spiritual or not. It can be part of a religious practice, or not. Although yoga is not religion by definition, it can be included in a religion as in Hinduism or Buddhism. Because of its age and vast diversity, yoga has no sole voice or singular expression.

For me, the practice of yoga is a spiritual practice. It helps me release my thoughts and engage my body so that I can connect with the best parts of who I am on a deeper level, all the while offering me physical fitness and stress relief. I still attend other teacher's classes, and I am constantly learning and growing. I am trying new styles, new postures and finding new ways of being with my practice and myself every day. You too can find your own path and cultivate what yoga might mean for you.

When I first came to this practice, I was stiff and had almost zero body awareness. Although I was fairly young when I found yoga, at almost six feet tall, I was not flexible. Hopefully, this will be inspiring for those of you that believe you must be young, flexible, strong, built like a dancer and look beautiful in expensive tight see-through yoga pants to practice yoga. I can promise you that when I started practicing yoga, I could not in fact touch my toes and I found any forward bending posture challenging. I was fairly self-conscious and I hated going to gyms. I think that I liked yoga so much at that point in time because I could hide in the back of a relatively darkened room and I didn't feel judged, gawked at or competed with. I felt more empowered with each new pose that I learned. In fact, I felt more myself and more natural than I had since I was a kid. Eventually, I built more self-confidence, centeredness and even flexibility. My body has changed in ways that I wouldn't have believed possible, as has my mind. The more I put into my practice, the greater the rewards have become. I did not originally come to yoga class with any expectation that it would change my life, but it did.

My progress at first was slow. I practiced yoga casually for several years, making it to classes when my schedule would allow. I now know that fifteen or twenty minutes every day is much more valuable than going to a one hour class once a week, although I push myself more in a class than I do on my own. Even more profound than the physical effects of flexibility, strength, general body awareness and stress relief, were the mental and psychological benefits. I have developed a mental peace through my practice, a sense of gratitude and a gradual and sometimes sudden opening of some formerly inflexible areas of my mind. Once I had developed a regular practice, I noticed a change in my outlook. Without even consciously trying, the calm that I experienced on the mat was spilling over into the rest of my life. I wanted to do more and more of what was giving me joy and helping me to create mental and physical space in my life. This desire to go deeper and learn more is what eventually led me to the Chopra Center, through certification and ultimately onto the path of teaching.

A Few Interesting Facts About Yoga

- Yoga originated in India roughly 3,000 years ago
- It is believed that there may be more people practicing yoga in California than in all of India
- An estimated 16 million people in North America practice yoga
- Male/Female breakdown - roughly 70% female/30% male
- Yoga can literally be done anywhere - variations can be done at your desk, in your car, or even on an airplane

Some Misconceptions About Yoga

- Yoga isn't only for the fit and flexible - some people avoid yoga because they think that they aren't cut out for Circ de Soleil, so why bother... If you fall into this category, then you probably NEED a yoga class.

- Yoga isn't a religion - Christians, Buddhists, Jews, Muslims, atheists, and agnostics alike practice yoga. As I mentioned above, there is certainly a spiritual side to yoga but you don't have to subscribe to any belief system to benefit.

- Yoga is not just a series of exercises, but also a vast system that includes physical postures that we call asanas as well as philosophies and techniques that help to bring the body, mind and spirit into balance naturally.

Few people know that the word yoga is a Sanskrit word that means union or yoking of the mind, body and spirit. Sanskrit is the oldest recorded language and originated in ancient India. Sanskrit has a unique sound vibration that resonates with the microcosm of our bodies and the macrocosm of the universe. Enlightened sages imparted it as a sublime sound system that would elevate one's consciousness. The vibrational power of this language is the reason that it is still used by yogis today.

You will notice that the Sanskrit names of yoga poses end in the word asana, which means pose, posture or seat. This is the most common use of the language, but it is also common to hear mantras like OM or shanti. In my personal practice, I chant the sun salutation mantras in Sanskrit. These words give thanks to the sun in all of its aspects, and the practice of making the sounds combined with the movements, strengthens my lungs, elevates my heart rate and clears my mind. Sound vibration can be very powerful and have profound effects on physiology and many yoga practitioners use chanting or sound vibration as a form of therapy.

Yoga, the art of right living was perfected and practiced in India thousands of years ago and the foundations of yoga philosophy were written down in *The Yoga Sutras* of Patanjali, in approximately 200 AD. A sutra is a thread or aphoristic (affirmational) verse. This ancient yet practical text describes the inner workings of the mind and provides an eight-step blueprint for controlling its restlessness so as to enjoy lasting peace. The basic questions - *who am I? where am I going? what is the purpose of life?* are asked by each new generation, and Patanjali answers. He explains what yoga is, how it works, and exactly how to purify the mind and let it settle into absolute stillness. The core of Patanjali's *Yoga Sutra* is an eight-limbed path that forms the structural framework for yoga practice. Upon practicing all eight limbs of the path it becomes self-evident that no one element is elevated over another in a hierarchical order. Each is part of a holistic focus, which eventually brings completeness to the individual as they find their connectivity to the divine. Because we are all uniquely individual a person can emphasize one branch and then move on to another as they round out their understanding. In brief the eight limbs, or steps to yoga, are as follows:

1. **Yama:** Universal morality (societal codes of conduct)
2. **Niyama:** Personal observances (personal codes of conduct)
3. **Asanas:** Body postures (yoga poses)
4. **Pranayama:** Breathing exercises, and control of prana (breath)
5. **Pratyahara:** Control of the senses (savasana)
6. **Dharana:** Concentration and cultivating inner perceptual awareness (present moment awareness)
7. **Dhyana:** Devotion and meditation on the Divine
8. **Samadhi:** Union with the Divine

The main takeaway here is that the practice of yoga is more than just a series of physical postures that we do in a class at the gym or the local yoga studio. It is part of a much larger system that includes codes of conduct or guidelines for living, breathing techniques, sense control, awareness, devotion and union. It is also important to understand that our bodies are more than just flesh and blood. There is more to us than meets the eye. As quantum physics has taught us, we are made up of energy, as is the entire universe. Once we recognize this and understand yoga's important teachings we can live the lives that we were meant to live.

Yogic Texts

If you want a deeper understanding of yoga, I recommend taking the time to read *The Yoga Sutras* by Patanjali as well as Dr. Deepak Chopra and Dr. David Simon's *The Seven Spiritual Laws of Yoga.* These two books will expand your understanding of the practice of yoga and help you to leverage the technologies available to unite your mind, body and spirit.

Know Thy Chakras, Know Thy Self

A more complete understanding of yoga will also include an understanding of the chakras, or energy centers in the body. There are seven major chakras or energy centers in the body and forty-three minor ones. These energy centers are junction points between consciousness and physiology; this is to say they are energetic, so you won't find them on an x-ray. They run along the spine from the tailbone to the crown of the head.

7 Main Energy Centers or Chakras

7th Chakra- Crown/ Sahaswahara
Color: Violet
Responsible for: Connection with higher self, the Divine and collective consciousness

6th Chakra- Third Eye/ Ajna
Color: Indigo
Responsible for: Intuition, Wisdom, Insight and vision

5th Chakra- Throat/ Vishuda
Color: Light Blue
Responsible for: Speech, authentic communication

4th Chakra- Heart/ Ajna
Color: Emerald Green
Responsible for: Love, emotion, connection, happiness

3rd Chakra- Solar Plexus/ Manipura
Color: Golden Yellow
Responsible for: Will, determination, manifestation, power

2nd Chakra- Sacral/ Svdisthana
Color: Orange
Responsible for: Creative and sexual energy, relationships

1st Chakra- Root (base of spine)/ Muladara
Color: Red
Responsible for: Basic needs, family, stability in life

Why is it important to understand this ancient and esoteric system? For me, learning about the chakras and their functions was like stepping into a whole new world. It wasn't until I connected with my own energy system that I truly understood my own body. When I started my journey like everyone else, I was living primarily in the first three energy centers, fulfilling base level functions with little awareness or consciousness. As I progressed along my path, things that felt nourishing at one point in time no longer made sense. As I connected more fully to my body, I felt more and more drawn to living a healthy lifestyle, cleaning out the clutter, and detoxing my life.

Through my yoga and meditation practice, I have learned to access and live in the higher chakras, enjoying their bliss and wisdom. Our bodies are full of wisdom. If we listen closely, our bodies will always tell us if we are making the most nourishing choice in every moment. For more information on chakras, I recommend reading *The Chakra Bible* by Patricia Mercier.

The chakra system is also connected to the different rooms in your home. Decluttering and cleaning each room can help to remove energetic blockages. Some examples follow. The living room is connected with the throat chakra because it is a place of communication and self-expression. The kitchen and dining room are connected with the heart chakra because they are places of pure unconditional love, devotion and gratitude. We will discuss each room and chakra connection more in depth along with natural cleaning recipes in chapter seven.

How the Chakras Apply to Your Home

Crown Chakra: attic and roof, including gutters
Third Eye Chakra: home office and windows
Throat Chakra: living room
Heart Chakra: kitchen and dining room
Solar Plexus Chakra: bathrooms
Sacral Chakra: bedrooms
Root Chakra: foundation and basement

As above, so below. As without, so within. Take a look at your home and then take a look at your body and your life. Are there any parallels? Are clutter, chaos, dust and debris in any room in your home pointing to any area in your body or in your life that needs attention? If something is not flowing in your life, start at home.

Many great teachers in history have taught their students to know themselves. Socrates taught his followers this. Ancient temples have these words inscribed over their doorways, and the famous poet Khalil Gibran said, *knowledge of the self is the mother of all knowledge. So it is incumbent on me to know myself, to know it completely, to know its minutiae, its characteristics, its subtleties, and its very atoms.* Awareness in the body is a good place to start. It is from this perspective that we can stay in present moment awareness and give our undivided attention to the task at hand. This is what yoga is - union or yoking of the mind, body and spirit. Yoga is body centered restful awareness and a powerful means for connecting to a more healthy and conscious way of living.

How to Practice Yoga

To really grasp what yoga can do, you need to experience it for yourself. There are many different styles and many forms of teaching. What you like and what is right for you is a matter of personal preference. Find what works best for you based on your fitness level or life needs. The following poses are essential basics that can be practiced easily in your own home. Start slowly and build from there. Just 15-20 minutes of yoga a day is preferred to just one hour per week. Yoga does not need to be complicated to be effective. It only needs to be performed consciously. When you are in a yoga pose, focus on your breathing. Bring awareness into your body, lengthening and deepening your breath. I would also recommend doing a few of these postures before beginning your cleaning routine in order to lubricate joints, keep your body flexible, and avoid injury. I have also included some additional poses for an extended routine and for variation, as well as some cool down and post cleaning poses.

- Pick up an inexpensive yoga mat.
- Find some stretchy, comfortable clothing that you can move in.

If you Choose to Go to a Yoga Class

- Choose a few classes that interest you, and try them out at your local yoga studio until you find a class and teacher that you like. Many studios will offer the first class for free.
- Turn off your cell phone before class. There is no bigger bummer than being interrupted in savasana by someone's cell phone ringing.
- Be sure to let your teacher know if you have any physical limitations or concerns. This can be the difference between having a horrible time and being comfortable enough to focus on your practice.

Try these basic poses in the comfort of your own home to get stronger and more flexible. There are variations in most yoga poses. Find the variation that works best for you. Because of ability and flexibility, your poses may look different than the pictures that follow. Move in the direction of flexibility and you will become more flexible.

Be gentle with yourself and start slowly.

Essential Basic Poses

Hands to Sky/Hasta Utanasana

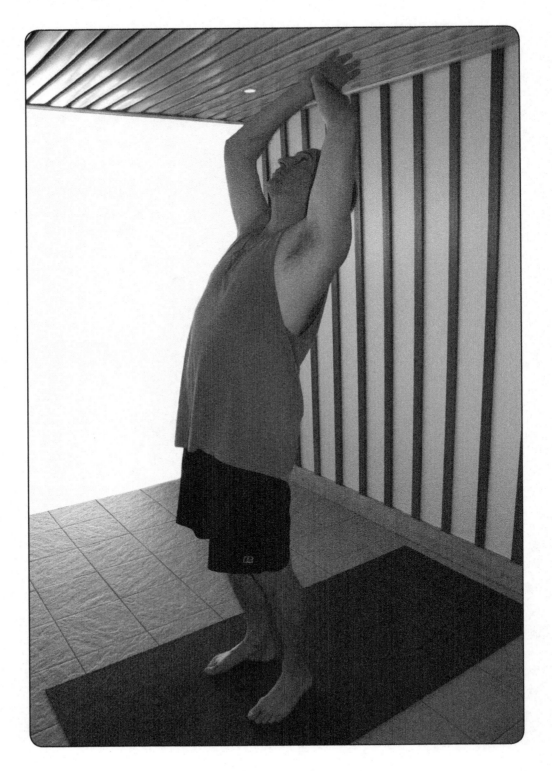

- Stand tall with feet together, shoulders relaxed, weight evenly distributed, arms at sides.
- Take a deep breath and raise your hands overhead, palms facing each other or with palms touching. Arms can be straight or bent as pictured. Reach up toward the sky with your fingertips.
- You can choose to create a slight back bend - looking up toward your thumbs as pictured or keep your spine straight and eyes forward.
- Hold for 3 to 5 deep breath cycles.

Benefits of Hands to Sky/Hasta Utanasana

- Strengthens and lengthens the legs, knees, ankles, arms, and chest
- Aligns spinal column and protects spinal muscles and nerves
- Creates space between vertebrae
- Prepares the spine for further stretching and flexing

Hands to Feet/Pada Hastasana

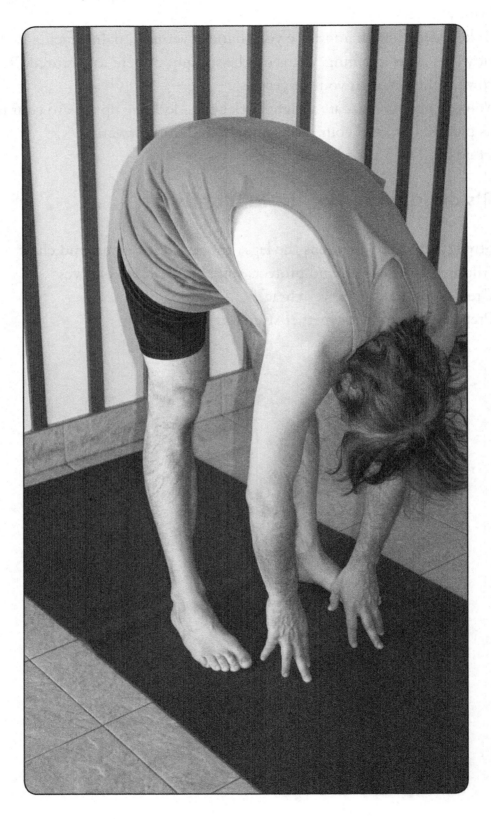

- On an exhale, bring your hands down to the sides of your feet bending your knees slightly. If your hamstrings are more flexible you can keep your knees straight and bend farther forward.
- Relax your head down. There should be no tension in you neck here.
- Hold for 3 to 5 deep breath cycles.

Benefits of Hands to Feet/Pada Hastasana

- Lengthens the spine and Increases flexibility
- Reduces pain in the lower back
- Improves flexibility of tendons and ligaments of the legs
- Opens shoulder joints
- Stimulates pituitary and pineal glands
- Exercises colon, pancreas and kidneys

Half Dog/Ardha Adho Mukha Svanasana

Achy back? Stiff legs? This is a good all around flexibility pose that can be done almost anywhere and is even gentle enough for pregnant women.

- Extend arms straight out from shoulders and place palms on wall. Walk feet back until arms and back are parallel to floor with legs directly under hips. Position feet parallel to each other and stretch toes.
- Hold for 5 to 10 deep breath cycles.

Benefits of Half Dog

- Strengthens the legs, knees, ankles, arms, and chest
- Releases low back pain
- Releases muscle tension due to stress
- An alternative to full downward facing dog for those with cardiovascular or neurologic conditions, such as hypertension or vertigo, also a great alternative for shoulder limitations
- An antidote stretch for working at a desk, driving or traveling

Triangle Pose/Trikonasana

Need to realign your spine or open up and stretch the psoas muscles located in the pelvic floor and inner thigh? If so, this is the pose for you. In my experience, people have a wide variety of ability in this pose based on shoulder and hip mobility. Ideally, you want the arms to be in one straight line up and down, the chest turning upward, the neck relaxed, the eyes upward. The hand can be on the leg, the ankle, a yoga block, or on the floor if you are really flexible. You want to make your body as flat as possible, imagining that you are between two sheets of glass.

- Stand straight. Separate your feet about hips width apart.
- Turn your right foot out 90 degrees and left foot in by 15 degrees.
- Now align the center of your right heel with the center of your left foot arch.
- Ensure that your feet are pressing into the floor and that the weight of your body is equally balanced on both feet.
- Inhale deeply and then on your exhale, bend your body to the right, downward from the hips, keeping the waist straight, allowing your left hand to come up in the air while your right hand comes down towards the floor. Keep both arms in a straight line.
- Rest your right hand on your shin, ankle, or the floor outside of your right foot; whatever is possible without distorting the sides of the waist. Stretch your left arm toward the ceiling, in line with the tops of your shoulders. Keep your head in a neutral position or turn it to the left, eyes gazing softly at the left palm.
- Stretch to your maximum limit and be steady. Keep taking in long deep breaths. With each exhalation, relax the body more and more. Just be with the body and the breath.
- Hold each side for 3 to 5 deep breath cycles.
- Repeat the same on the other side.

Benefits of Triangle Pose:

- Promotes flexibility and toning of the thigh muscles
- Improves flexibility in the spine and can correct shoulder alignment
- Strengthens the knees and ankles
- Tones the arms
- Strengthens the neck
- Massages abdominal organs
- Improves balance
- Relieves stress
- Improves circulation

Tree Pose/Vrksasana

Balance poses have an amazing capacity to ground us and keep us focused in present moment awareness. It's tough to think about chores, responsibilities and how clean the house is when you are focused on not falling over.

- Stand straight with your arms by your sides. Shift your weight entirely onto the left foot, keeping the entire foot flat on the floor. Bend your right knee. If you are new to balancing postures you can let your toes touch the floor while you balance predominately on your left foot. If you are ready for the full expression of the pose, reach down with your right hand and clasp your right ankle.

- Draw your right foot up and place the sole against the inner left thigh; if possible, press the right heel into the inner left groin, toes pointing toward the floor. The center of your pelvis should be directly over the left foot. The foot can be placed on the inner thigh, the calf, or against the ankle with the toe touching the floor. Avoid placing the foot on the knee as this can cause unnecessary stress to the joint.

- Rest your hands on the top rim of your pelvis. Make sure the pelvis is in a neutral position, with the top rim parallel to the floor.

- Lengthen your tailbone toward the floor. Firmly press the right foot sole against the inner thigh and resist with the outer left leg. Variations include hands together in prayer pose, arms extended like tree branches or palms together overhead in temple pose. Gaze softly at a fixed point in front of you.

- Stay for 30 seconds to 1 minute breathing deeply.

- Release the foot and come back to a normal standing posture with an exhalation and then repeat on the other side.

Benefits of Tree Pose

- Improves balance and stability in the legs
- Strengthens the ligaments and tendons of the feet
- Strengthens the entire leg up to the buttocks
- Assists the body in establishing pelvic stability
- Strengthens the hip bones

Additional Poses for Variation and Extended Practice

Sun Salutations/Surya Namaskar

The following sequence is as taught by the Chopra Center and is part of the *The Seven Spiritual Laws of Yoga* program. This sequence is practiced like a dance - meaning one pose flows into the next. There are many variations of sun salutations but I find this sequence more nourishing and challenging than other variations that I have tried. You will begin by moving through the out cycle with the left leg back and then in the return cycle with the left leg forward and then switch sides. Practicing just 4-6 rounds balances each side of the body and will target every major muscle group, serving as a complete workout in itself.

1. Salutation Pose/Pranamasana

- Palms are touching at heart center.
- Stand with feet, and thighs touching and spine straight.
- Hold for 3 to 5 deep breath cycles.

2. Hands to Sky Pose/Hasta Uttanasana

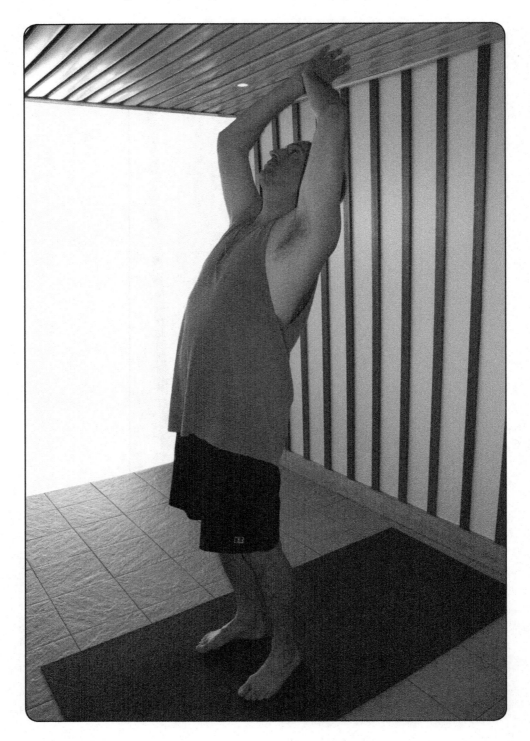

- Inhaling, extend arms in an arc over head, reaching your hands toward the sky.
- Relax shoulders down and away from the ears. Look up towards your thumbs.

3. Hands to Feet Pose/Pada Hastasana

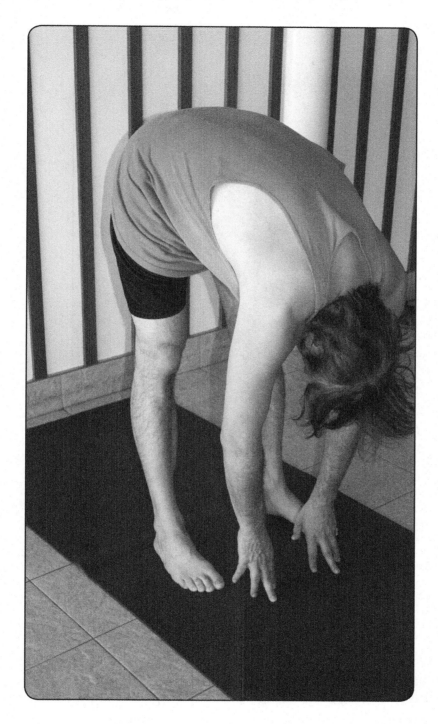

- Exhale, bringing your hands down to the sides of your feet, bending your knees slightly.
- Relax your head down.

4. Equestrian Pose/Ashwa Sanchalanasana

- Inhaling, extend your left leg back, bending your right knee.
- Curl your back toes under and lightly rest the top part of your left knee on the floor for balance.
- Make sure your right knee is in line and slightly over the right ankle (think stability). Raise your arms over head with hands and face to the sky.

5. Mountain Pose (Downward Facing Dog)/Parvatasana

- Exhale and bring your right leg back parallel to your left leg.
- Lift your tailbone up toward the sky and relax your head down between your arms.
- Heels are pressed down toward, or on the floor if possible.

6. Eight Limbs Pose/Asthanga Namaskar

- Inhaling, curl your toes coming down to your knees and sweep the body down onto the chest and chin. The chin, chest and knees touch the mat and the hips are lifted. This pose is called eight limbs because eight parts of the body are touching the mat - the chin, chest, hands, knees and feet.
- Fingertips are aligned with the shoulders.
- Arms are by your sides, elbows in and up toward the sky slightly and shoulders are rolled back and down - away from the ears.

7. Cobra Pose/Bhujangasana

- Inhale and lift up into cobra by pushing off the mat with your arms.
- Keep your shoulders rolled back and down - away from the ears.
- Elbows will be slightly bent with arms by your sides or fully extended for variation.
- Lift your face toward the sky.
- Make sure your legs are together with the tops of your feet on the floor.

Return Cycle

8. Mountain Pose (Downward Facing Dog) / Parvatasana

- Exhale and curl your toes forward to lift your tailbone toward the sky.
- Relax your head in between your arms.
- Heels are pressed down toward, or on the floor if possible.

9. Equestrian Pose/Ashwa Sanchalanasana

- Inhaling, bring your left forward between your hands, bending your left knee.
- Curl your back toes under and lightly rest the top part of your right knee on the floor for balance or lift the knee off the floor and balance on the back toes for variation.
- Make sure your right knee is in line and slightly over the right ankle (think stability). Raise your arms over head with hands and face to the sky.

10. Hands to Feet Pose/Pada Hastasana

- Exhale and gently bring your right foot forward to standing forward bend with hands down to the side of your feet, bending your knees slightly.
- Relax your head down.

11.   Hands to Sky Pose/Hasta Uttanasana

- Inhaling, roll up one vertebra at a time. Head is the last to come up.
- Extend arms over head, reaching your hands toward the sky.
- Relax shoulders down and away from the ears. Lift your face toward the sky.

12. Salutation Pose/Pranamasana

- Exhaling, bring the palms back to heart center.
- Stand with feet, and thighs touching, spine straight.
- Hold for 3 to 5 deep breath cycles.

Benefits of Sun Salutations

- Strengthens the heart
- Improves circulation
- Lengthens and strengthens all major muscles in the body

Cool Down Sequence

Cobra Pose/Bhugangasana

- Lie down on your abdomen and point your feet behind you. Place your hands palms down on the floor beneath your shoulders.
- Bring your hands underneath your shoulders as you lift your head up off the floor by straightening your arms. Engage your gluteal (butt) and back muscles as you curl your chest away from the floor.
- Gaze upwards and keep your abdominals engaged.

Benefits of Cobra Pose

- Stretches muscles in the shoulders, chest and abdominals
- Decreases stiffness in the lower back
- Strengthens the arms and shoulders
- Increases flexibility
- Elevates mood
- Massages abdominal organs
- Strengthens the spine

Head to Knee Pose/Janu Sirsasana

- Sit on the floor with your legs straight in front of you or on a folded blanket if your hamstring muscles are especially tight. Inhale, bend your right knee and draw the right heel back toward your inner thigh. Rest your right foot sole lightly against your inner left thigh and lay the outer right leg on the floor with the shin at a right angle to the left leg. If your right knee doesn't rest comfortably on the floor, support it with a folded blanket.

- Press your right hand against the inner right groin where the thigh joins the pelvis and put your left hand on the floor beside the hip. Exhale and turn the torso slightly to the left, lifting the torso as you push down on the inner right thigh. Line up your navel with the middle of the left thigh. For variation, you can use a strap to help you lengthen the spine evenly, grounding through the sitting bones.

- When you are ready, reach out with your right hand to take the inner left foot. Inhale and lift the front torso, pressing the top of the left thigh into the floor and extending actively through the left heel. Use the pressure of the left hand on the floor to increase the twist to the left. Then reach your left hand to the outside of the foot. With the arms fully extended, lengthen the front torso from the pubis to the top of the sternum.

- Exhale and extend forward from the groin, not the hips. Be sure not to pull yourself forcefully into the forward bend, hunching the back and shortening the front torso. As you descend, bend your elbows out to the sides and lift them away from the floor.
- Lengthen forward into a comfortable stretch. The lower belly should touch the thighs first, the head last. Stay in the pose anywhere from 1 to 3 minutes. Come up with an inhalation and repeat the pose on the other side.

Benefits of Head to Knee Pose

- Calms the mind and relieves mild depression
- Stretches the spine, shoulders, hamstrings, and groin
- Therapeutic for high blood pressure, insomnia, and sinusitis

Seated Forward Bend/Paschimottanasana

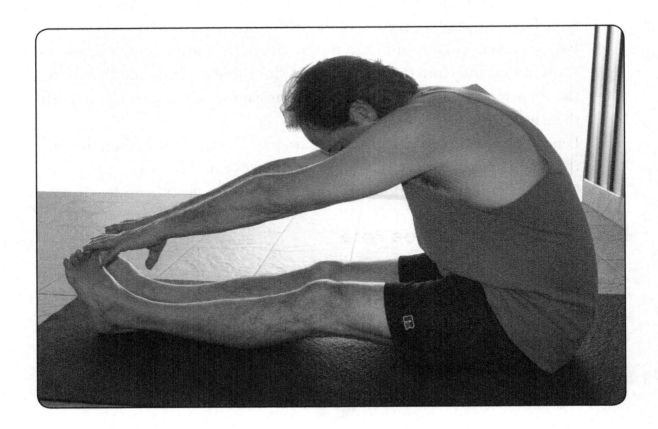

- Sit on the floor or with your buttocks supported on a folded blanket and your legs straight in front of you. Press actively through your heels. Rock slightly onto your left buttock and pull your right sitting bone away from the heel with your right hand. Repeat on the other side.
- Draw the inner groins deep into the pelvis. Inhale and keeping the front torso long, lean forward from the hip joints, not the waist. Lengthen the tailbone away from the back of your pelvis. If possible take the sides of the feet with your hands, elbows fully extended. If this isn't possible, loop a strap around the feet and hold the strap firmly. Be sure your elbows are straight, not bent.
- When you are ready to go further, don't forcefully pull yourself into the forward bend whether your hands are on the feet or holding the strap. Always lengthen the front torso into the pose, keeping your head raised. If you are holding the feet, bend the elbows out to the sides and lift them away from the floor; if holding the strap, lighten your grip and walk the hands forward,

keeping the arms long. The lower belly should touch the thighs first, then the upper belly, then the ribs and the head last.

- With each inhalation, lift and lengthen the front torso just slightly; with each exhalation release a little more fully into the forward bend. In this way the torso oscillates and lengthens almost imperceptibly with the breath. Eventually you may be able to stretch the arms out beyond the feet on the floor.

- Stay in the pose anywhere from 1 to 3 minutes. To come up, first lift the torso away from the thighs and straighten the elbows again if they are bent. Then inhale and lift the torso up by pulling the tailbone down and into the pelvis.

Benefits of Seated Forward Bend

- Lengthens, tones and flexes the spine
- Relieves constipation and promotes digestion
- Strengthens the pancreas

Corpse Pose/Savasana

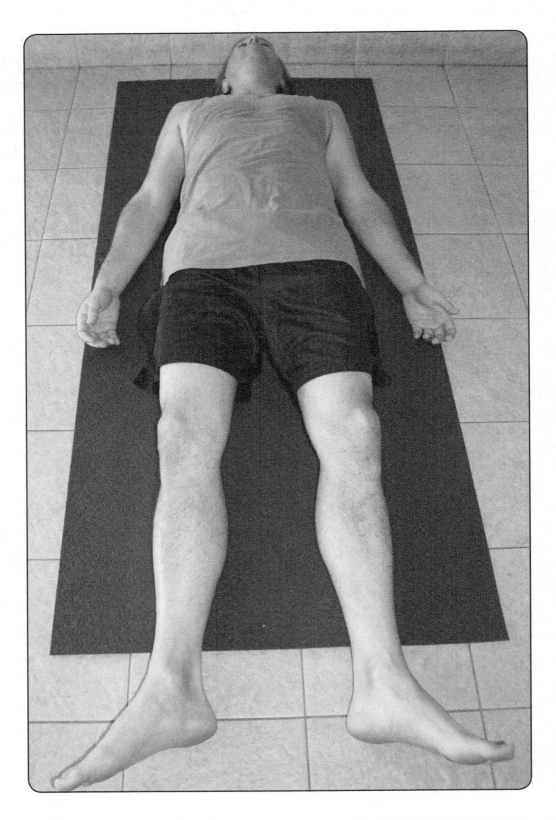

- In a reclined position, extend the arm and legs on the floor and let the feet drop out to the side. Palms are facing up, eyes are gently closed.
- Press down with your elbows and bring your shoulders back and down. Relax.
- Soften the tongue and gently part the lips.
- Lengthen and deepen the breath and just surrender to the pose.
- Stay in this pose for 5 minutes for every 30 minutes of practice.
- To exit, first roll gently with an exhalation onto one side, preferably the right. Take 2 or 3 breaths. With another exhalation press your hands against the floor and lift your torso, dragging your head slowly after. The head should always come up last.

Benefits of Corpse Pose

- Calms the mind
- Relaxes the body
- Reduces stress and mild depression
- Reduces headache, fatigue, and insomnia
- Helps lower blood pressure

3 Cleaning Is Well-being

Housekeeping ain't no joke
~ Louisa May Alcott

A clean house is more than just preferable - it's a necessity for good mental and physical health. Experts agree that maintaining a regular cleaning schedule is just as important as eating healthy food, exercising and taking vitamins. According to Wikipedia, *cleanliness is both the abstract state of being clean and free from dirt and the process of achieving and maintaining that state*. Cleanliness may be endowed with a moral quality, as indicated by the aphorism *cleanliness is next to godliness*.

Our homes are a reflection of our well-being. The way we use, care for and create space activates energy and helps us establish a nourishing environment for healthy, harmonious lives. We need to feel safe at home. A clean, appealing home, no matter how small, can become a special space for you to recharge your batteries, connect with your loved ones, or create something magical like a garden or a lovely meal. Think of your clearing, cleaning, and purifying as part of the sacred act and art of living.

Cleaning is Not for Wimps

Not to freak you out or anything, but there are roughly more than 500,000 bacteria living in your kitchen. Countertops, sinks, drains, sponges and floors are home to thousands of germs and bacteria. There are more bacteria living in your shower than in the garbage can. The good news is that the germs and viruses come off our body when we bathe. The bad news is that they stay in the shower until it's disinfected because moisture goes with germs like peanut butter goes with jelly. If that's not enough to convince you, the US Occupational Safety and Health Administration reports that dust buildup can contribute to poor indoor air quality which has been tied to causing headaches, difficulty with concentration and irritation of the eyes, nose, throat, and lungs. Cleaning the house is serious business and needs to be done on a regular basis to keep germs at bay and health in balance.

Cleaning Can Provide a Sense of Well-being

Health factors aside, there are other reasons why cleaning is so vital. One reason is a sense of satisfaction with a job well done. The joy of cleaning comes with a tangible result. The house is clean, uncluttered, germ-free and smelling good. This small achievement can spill over into other areas of our lives, giving us the confidence that we can tackle a project and succeed. We may not be able to directly control the economy, the boss's mood, or world peace, but we do have control over having a clean sink or a clean house.

Cleaning can also be calming to the mind. Cleaning up our external environment can make us feel like we're cleaning up our psyche. It feels good to clean the past week of old energy and debris so that we can start the week ahead fresh and new. And who would not benefit from a little meditation in the form of a mindless task to reduce the stress of living a busy life in a fast-paced world? I actually find cleaning to be a relaxing activity - whether I listen to an audio book, music, repeat a mantra or just shut off my mind completely focusing on the task at hand. No matter how much change occurs in my life, the need to clean is consistent and that is somehow reassuring.

Cleaning is a Mood-Boosting Workout

Cleaning burns calories - roughly 170 per hour for a moderate effort and more than 200 for a vigorous routine. Research also shows that it can increase endorphins (feel good hormones in the body). A 2008 study conducted by the British Journal of Sports Medicine found that just 20 minutes of sustained exercise a week such as cleaning could improve your mood and lift depression. The more strenuous and frequent the activity the greater the effect. Running up and down the stairs, carrying items from room to room and scrubbing windows and floors can burn calories, release endorphins, and help you blow off steam. Spring cleaning is a workout routine that brings many benefits indeed.

Why We Clean

Based on research, there are four main reasons why people clean. They like it, they have to, there is an event or there is a life stage change.

People Clean Because They Like It

Believe it or not, 55% of men and 62% of women claim to receive a sense of satisfaction from cleaning. I have sat in on focus groups where women describe a scene where they send their husband and/or children out for the afternoon so that they can put on some music, get out all the cleaning supplies and seriously clean the house. They describe cleaning the house from top to bottom for hours. Some of them even enjoy a glass of wine while doing so. Most of them use harsh chemicals so that the house smells like Pine Sol and bleach. One woman said that she didn't believe the house was really clean unless her eyes were burning. Yikes.

Another reason many may feel so connected to cleaning is that it provides a focused and repetitious task. The task of cleaning is a vehicle to get you out of your mind and the details of your life, into your body and the job at hand - a sort of moving meditation leaving you more relaxed after you finish. Playing your favorite music as you clean may also make the work faster and more enjoyable.

People Clean Because They Have to

26% of men and women say that cleaning is a thankless chore. Based on research, half of these people are cleaning for the sake of their children and the other half are cleaning for the sake of their significant other. We're busy and we don't have the right tools so doing it all easily overwhelms us. If we don't have two hours to devote to the project then maybe we don't even try. The house gets dirtier and dirtier until eventually, the smells, dirty clothes and the stacks of mail pile up until we MUST do something about it. Whether you love it or hate it, cleaning really is an unavoidable task. Clutter can create stress to the point that you don't even want to come home. Or worse, the bacteria can become harmful and unsanitary.

People Clean Because There is an Event (Guest/Holiday)

A wide majority - 82% of women say that they're driven to clean when anticipating guests. You know the old saying, if you want the house neat and clean just invite some people over. The anxiety of having people in your home puts on the pressure to get the place clean. This is also known as crisis cleaning. We have all experienced it. The sudden phone call that says people are coming over. The best course of action for a last minute houseguest is to *fake* clean. This is not the time for detailed housework. This is the time to stash the clutter and get the surfaces clear (just the parts that your guests can see). Lighting a scented candle can have a quick impact on the mood in the space and can help keep you present in the face of potential chaos.

People Clean Because There is a Life Change (Pets/Children/Health/Moving)

Life change events can elevate the importance of cleaning. Some 81% of women age 35-44 report that having a child has increased the importance of cleaning. For 53% buying a new home made cleaning more important.

Dusting, mopping and vacuuming - that's easy. Getting rid of all the junk you have to dust, mop and vacuum around? Not so much. *Giving things up is tough because it's not so clear-cut when they're no longer useful,* says Julie Morgenstern, author of *Shed Your Stuff, Change Your Life.* You don't stop wearing jeggings (jean leggings) on a Tuesday at 4 p.m.; you just gradually stop doing so, even as they languish on a hanger. Some motivations to get going on cleaning house include - a new baby, a new puppy, buying or selling a house or a major health concern. Any of these factors would greatly impact your need to minimize, reorganize and clean house.

How To Get Motivated to Clean

Most of us really do enjoy having clean homes, but sometimes we just need a little motivation.

- Put on some good music - something upbeat that you love and can move to. Make a housecleaning play list.
- Pour yourself a glass of something and stay hydrated.
- Dress the part. Put on comfy, stretchy clothes or a French Maid outfit.
- Stretch your body to prevent injury.
- Set a timer and clear and clean what you can in the allotted time.
- Ask for help. Divide up cleaning chores.
- Put on the pressure if needed - invite someone over for dinner. The fear of having someone judge you for being untidy is motivation enough for anyone.

How To Make Cleaning More Yogic

These ideas are an invitation, not an obligation. Have fun with it.

- Clean and clear your space with intention and presence for the greatest good of all concerned.
- Recite a mantra like OM or Shanti (peace) or whatever you choose.
- Repeat an affirmation like:

*I clean and clear this place. Only good is
welcome here, this is sacred space.*

- Dedicate your act of cleaning to all beings or to someone in particular.
- See your cleaning practice as a form of karma yoga or selfless service.
- Practice bhakti yoga by carrying a loving intention for yourself, your family and your home.

4 Just Breathe

Deep breaths are very helpful at shallow parties.
~ Barbara Walters

In yoga, breath is called pranayama - a Sanskrit word meaning *extension of the life force*. Wherever you are now, sitting or standing, take a deep breath and let it out with a sigh. Notice how you are feeling. Do it again. Breathe deep and follow the exhale with an audible sigh. Notice how you feel now. Any difference? Do you feel more relaxed now? I often tell my yoga students that breath is the greatest teacher and that I am merely their guide.

Notice your breath now. Are you holding it? Are you taking emaciated and shallow breaths? Is your breathing heavy and labored? Putting awareness on the breath is a good way to gage where we are in the present moment. Ask yourself, am I in balance? We unconsciously hold our breath many times each day. In fact, this is usually the first thing that we do when we don't want to lose control of some situation. This is part of a normal reflex that we have that causes us to tense up and "get through it" when we should be doing the exact opposite. We have reduced our breathing to a survival level. We take in just enough oxygen to stay alive. Vigorous exercise or a thorough house cleaning may be the only times when we truly breathe deeply. Studies have shown that oxygen can trick cells into believing that they are younger than they are. In short, breath allows rejuvenation to occur.

Since breathing is something we can control and regulate, it is a useful tool for achieving a relaxed and clear state of mind. The following three breathing exercises will help you relax and reduce stress. These exercises are utterly simple, take almost no time, require no equipment and can be done anywhere. These are my go-to breaths for almost any situation - belly breathing, rhythmatic breathing, and alternate nostril breathing. Try each and see how they affect your stress and anxiety levels. I find these simple breathing techniques to be the most helpful and useful of all of the different types of breathing methods that I have learned and tried myself. They are also the easiest to perform. I use these techniques on a regular basis in my yoga practice and in my own life.

Belly Breathing

This is a core breath that I use at the beginning of almost all of my yoga classes. This is helpful for bringing awareness into the body and calming the mind.

- Gently close your eyes and sit comfortably or lie down with the spine straight. Relax your hands in your lap or rest your arms next to your side with the palms facing up.
- Inhale through the nose and allow the belly to expand.
- Exhale through the nose and allow the belly to lower.

When you think about the belly or abdomen expanding, think about a balloon as it expands. With awareness on the breath and body in this specific way, the breath should be deeper and more elongated. I use this breath when I want to relax or let go of my thoughts.

Variations

- Visualize a tube running from the top of your head to the base of your spine.
- Inhale through the nose and allow white light energy to enter the tube at the top of your head and flow down the tube and out at the base of the spine.
- Exhale through the nose and allow the white light energy to enter the tube at the base of the spine and flow upward and out at the top of your head.
Or
- Visualize your body filling with white light as you inhale and exhale from the belly center as the belly expands and contracts.

Rhythmatic Breathing

This is a more energizing breath. Use this if you are feeling sluggish or disconnected from your body or need more energy. You may attract attention if you do this in an office setting.

- Eyes can be open or closed. You can be sitting or standing. I usually perform this breath while standing, kneeling or walking.
- Inhale through the nose twice in quick short succession.
- Exhale through the nose twice in quick short succession.
- Repeat. That's it. Inhale, inhale, exhale, exhale.

You will feel more energized after just 6 in and out cycles of the breath. Pause between cycles with a regular inhale and exhale. This will keep you from becoming light headed. This breath will turn routine activities into a moving meditation and makes mundane cleaning tasks more fun. I use this breath to create energy instead of going for another cup of coffee. I often use this breath when folding laundry.

Variations

- To get heart rate up even higher, pump arms up and down or in and out in rhythm with the breath.
- Use this breath to quickly bring movement into the spine. While seated or kneeling on the floor, place hands on knees and on the inhale move the torso forward, creating a gentle back bend. On the exhale move the torso backward creating a gentle forward bend.

Alternate Nostril Breathing/Nodi Shodhana

This breath is great for releasing tension and balancing the left and right hemispheres of the brain. Try this breath before meditating or just before going to sleep. It helps to quiet the mind.

- Sit comfortably with spine erect. Eyes can be open or closed.
- Gently rest the first two fingers of the right hand on your forehead - just between your eyebrows.
- Place the thumb of your right hand on you right nostril, closing it off.
- Inhale through your left nostril and hold the breath for just a moment. The mouth should be closed.
- Cover and hold the left nostril with the ring or fourth finger on your right hand.
- Release your thumb and exhale the breath through your right nostril.
- Inhale again through your right nostril while your fourth finger closes your left nostril.
- Cover and hold the right nostril with your thumb while you release your fourth finger from your left nostril and exhale.
- Repeat for as long as you like going back and forth as described above.

There are no variations to this breath. I use this when I have a headache or sinus trouble.

Simply put, bringing awareness to the breath brings awareness to the body. Bringing awareness to the body takes the awareness off the mind. Taking awareness off the mind means stopping the incessant mind chatter that slowly drives us all mad and deepens our stress levels. Lowering stress levels means boosting the immune system. Doing this as much as possible will help to eliminate stress, slow down aging and prevent illness. Use your breath.

A Word on Meditation

We live in a fast paced world and most of us stay in "fight or flight" mode all the time. In this state of awareness cortisol levels stay high. Cortisol is a useful stress hormone when trying to escape from a bear or some other similar situation but it keeps the immune system suppressed. This is part of the reason why we are the most sick and overweight population ever. A good meditation practice can have profound effects on the nervous system and on all of the bodily systems, helping to reduce cortisol levels to normal and boosting immune function.

There are many studies available on the benefits of meditation. In 2012, a study found that participating in an 8-week meditation training program can have measurable effects on how the brain functions even when someone is not actively meditating. In their report in the November issue of *Frontiers in Human Neuroscience*, investigators at Massachusetts General Hospital, Boston University and several other research centers found differences in those effects based on the specific type of meditation practiced. The group that practiced mindful or focused attention on a task like cleaning or folding laundry, showed a decrease in response to all stressful images, supporting the hypothesis that meditation can improve emotional stability and response to stress.

For years, meditators have said that the practice keeps them healthy. Another study, published in the journal *Circulation: Cardiovascular Quality and Outcomes* actually tested this. 201 people with coronary heart disease were asked to either (a) take a health education class promoting better diet and exercise or (b) take a class on transcendental meditation. Researchers followed up with participants for the next five years and found that those who took the meditation class had a 48% reduction in their overall risk of heart attack, stroke and death. It's an initial study, but a promising one.

There are plenty of tools available for meditation. This is an intimidating concept for some people and completely foreign to others. It's really not that complicated. Most people assume that meditation is all about stopping thoughts, getting rid of emotions and somehow controlling the mind. Actually, it's much different than that. It's more about stepping back and seeing the thought clearly - witnessing it coming and going without judgment and with a relaxed, focused mind.

Cleaning as a Form of Meditation

Make your cleaning routine a meditation. Focus intently on what you are doing - i.e., folding a pair of socks or mopping the floor. Think of nothing else except for that task. This can be challenging, as thoughts will try to dominate your attention. You have a lot of things to get done and little time to do them, but you can use these routine cleaning tasks as an opportunity to release stress, focus your attention and create space in your mind. Give it a try and you might be surprised at just how calming it can be once you get the hang of it. I often do this in my own life. I just surrender to the task at hand and devote my entire energetic life force to it. This can be extremely relaxing and it is often at moments like this that I have a sudden inspiration, idea or solution to a problem that had previously been eluding me. Surrendering to the task at hand can be very rewarding.

I would like to give props to Electrolux the vacuum cleaner company for seeing the connection between cleaning and well-being in a way that you would least expect. Their proposition for a product called *Clean Your Mind* is that vacuuming takes an average of 15 minutes and you can transfer that time slot from a necessary chore into a 15 minute resource for your own well-being. Train your brain while you are vacuuming with the first meditation program developed for vacuum cleaning. You can download or stream *Clean Your Mind* from iTunes or Spotify. This concept gives multi-tasking a whole new meaning. You could download any guided meditation in fact or just listen to calming music while you clean. The idea here is to release resistance and gain the benefits of stress relief.

How to Meditate

Find a quiet place where you won't be disturbed. I recommend meditation first thing in the morning, following a trip to the bathroom. Depending on how much time I have, I meditate daily for between 15-30 minutes. I personally use a mantra or Sanskrit sound that creates vibration in combination with prayer and visualization. If at all possible, find a teacher to help you get your practice started. Here are some other options:

- Use a guided meditation - this is a nice way to get started. Downloads are available on chopra.com, iTunes, hayhouseradio.com and other places online. Find a teacher and a style that resonates with you.
- Use a mantra like SO HUM. Just repeat the mantra SO HUM over and over quietly in your mind. This translates to I am that/I am the universe. When thoughts creep in, just go back to the mantra. Loose yourself in the sound vibration of the mantra.
- Listen intently to chilled out meditation music like *MEDITATE* or *RELAX* by my husband and New Age Artist Paul Avgerinos and deepen your breath while you do so.
- Focus only on your breath flowing in and out of your body.
- Focus intently on your activity with mindful attention.

5 Declutter

A house is just a pile of stuff with a cover on it.
~ George Carlin
Clutter-clearing is modern-day alchemy.
~ Denise Linn

There is nothing spiritual, helpful or healthy about clutter. Clutter is restrictive and heavy. It carries a negative energy all its own. The burden of clutter becomes obvious when your home or personal space is so oppressive that you don't want to be in it. When you sell, give away or throw out your clutter, you then realize just how emotionally and physically draining it has been.

Clearing clutter is one of the greatest ways to boost your energy, get yourself out of a rut, feel lighter, remove obstacles and create space for the new to arrive. Clearing clutter is a proven therapy for creating change in your life. *Now* is always the perfect time for a focused clutter clearing session.

I was a big fan of the TLC (The Learning Channel) TV show *Clean Sweep*. The show featured organizational expert Peter Walsh and a crew who helped homeowners clear and redecorate one or two rooms of clutter in a two-day process. It was truly amazing to see inside of people's homes and how much stuff they had! Some of the people on the show had so much stuff in their homes that entire rooms were completely unusable. In each episode, the host met with the homeowners in the rooms to be cleared. The production crew then moved the entire contents of the rooms outdoors. The host then assisted the homeowners to sort all the items into three areas - keep, sell or toss. The process was then repeated by Walsh, in a much more thorough manner. Meanwhile, the designer and carpenter renovated the rooms, usually painting and constructing storage units such as closets, entertainment units or cabinets. On the second day, a yard sale was held to dispose of the items in the sell category. The homeowners, usually a husband and wife team, competed to sell the most, with the loser having to give up a sentimental item from the keep category. Once the rooms were renovated and the remaining items from the keep category were moved back into the house, the homeowners were brought back in to be surprised by the final results. They couldn't believe that they had let their "stuff" take over their lives. There would often be a moment when Walsh would have to talk one or both of the people off the ledge in order to help them let go of something. They usually cried because they were so overwhelmed by the beautiful and usable space that they could now enjoy. I loved that show.

Excessive clutter and disorganization are often symptoms of bigger problems. At its most extreme, chronic disorganization is called hoarding. A condition many experts believe is a mental illness in its own right, although psychiatrists have yet to formally recognize it. It's not clear how many people suffer from compulsive hoarding, but estimates start at about 1.5 million. Often, the clutter stems from an emotional cause. The following are the seven most common excuses that people use to keep their clutter. Do any of these sound familiar?

It was a gift from _____ (insert name)

Presents and gifts hiding around your house that are not loved or used can be classified as clutter. You simply feel obliged to keep them. You don't throw them out because you might feel guilty.

I might use that again at some point

You keep all kinds of stuff just in case. Just in case you might need it someday. Just in case you couldn't afford to buy another one in the future, just in case you might read it sometime soon, just in case you lose weight or just in case for no particular reason. The fact that you haven't used it in 2, 3 or 15 years generally means its once useful purpose has expired.

I don't feel like dealing with my stuff

People with depression tend to have a lot of things stored on the floor. Stuff on the floor pulls your energies down and encourages you to withdraw from the world emotionally. If your floor is covered with lots of stuff, make an effort each day to start picking things up. I guarantee it won't be long until you start noticing a difference in your moods and how your home feels.

It was on sale!

Buying stuff to make you feel happy again is a quick fix solution. It does not bring deep long lasting satisfaction to your life and the item you bought only brings happiness momentarily. Compulsive buying without any thought and addiction to sales and bargains simply adds to the congestion and confusion already filling your home and life. Take an honest look at your stuff and see if you have any addiction clutter floating around. Better still; never go shopping without a list. Consciously choose what you intend to bring into your home and for every new item purchased throw out at least one or two. Keep the energy flowing.

It might be worth something

You feel that your sense of self worth is reflected by the appearance or value of the stuff in your living space. You generally don't like many of your possessions but have them because they are the latest trend, most impressive or even the most expensive. Filling your home with stuff to impress your ego or others simply means you are out of alignment with your life and the energy in your home. This can be as obvious as a bookcase full of books that you never look at or even care about. It only gives the impression that you are well read and knowledgeable.

I don't like change

If you are scared of change then you will have denial clutter. You have a sense that your world may fall apart if you start removing serious amounts of clutter from your home. You may be consistent in throwing out surface clutter but when it comes to a serious clutter busting session to invite wonderful change you consistently tell yourself that this item or that possession is not clutter. Yes, it is.

I'm just storing it for a friend

When you look after stuff for other people get clear with how long you are minding it for. Short term is generally fine as you are being helpful. If however their stuff turns into annoyance or frustration then your act of kindness has evolved into energy draining clutter that's not even yours. Your friends or family need to find other arrangements or put it in storage.

Clutter and the Chakras

Chakra blockages are often mirrored by the state of disarray in various rooms in your home. A person does not have to look beyond their own home environment to discover which chakra centers may be problematic or blocked. Hoarders are especially at risk of a complete chakra system shutdown. To clear your energy body, it is important that you do the work of decluttering. Of course, you can certainly ask for help. As you sort out your stuff, you will begin to clear your energy body and your entire life will benefit.

How to Declutter

Clearing clutter moves you forward. If you are reading this book, you clearly are ready to have more peace and well-being in your life. It's all up to you. Here are some suggestions on how to "get-er-done."

Start Small

Pick a drawer, a closet or a room and systematically go through it. Consider every item. Do you need it? Do you love it? Will you use it? A good guideline is that if you haven't needed it or worn it in two years, you should sell it, toss it or give it away.

In the Northeast, most people need to store clothing for the off-season. This gives us an opportunity to review and purge items that we no longer use or that are damaged. Create a toss, keep, and donate pile with clothes, shoes and accessories before storing them away for the season. Also, refrain from purchasing new stuff until you have unpacked stored items for the new season. People often forget what they already have. For the items that you have determined that you really need to keep, consider if you need additional storage – shelving, containers, bins, etc.

Commit to Clean

Short on time? Avoid having to overhaul a space by spending 10-15 minutes a day straightening and decluttering the entire house or just one room at a time. Set a timer so that you don't get lost in the weeds. Go through each room or one room a day and scan for misplaced items that can be put away or thrown out. Don't let stuff get stacked up. This will create more work later on. Putting things back in their place will also save time when you need to find them.

Go for the Gusto

If you are someone who needs a little motivation to get things done, there is nothing like the added pressure of impending houseguests. Plan a party or invite the in-laws over to stay. This will force you to clean the crap out of the guest room. This is an aspect of the ego that is actually useful. Most people do not want to be seen as sloppy or unclean. Go through the space and put things in groups - keep, toss, give away or sell. Plan a tag or garage sale. If you need help getting organized, call for reinforcements. Sometimes it can be difficult to do the larger jobs on your own or be objective about what you should keep. Don't be afraid to ask for help, hire a professional, or barter with a friend. Your life and the energy in your home should feel lighter after the clutter has been cleared. Cortisol levels will lower returning your immune system to healthy function. Cleaning and energy work will finish the job. We will discuss these in the next chapters.

6 The Cleaning Routine

*Laughter and tears are both responses
to frustration and exhaustion.
I myself prefer to laugh, since there is less
cleaning up to do afterward.*
~ Kurt Vonnegut

Now that the clutter is cleared, we can get down to the business of cleaning. This can be an enjoyable and rewarding experience, even stress relieving as mentioned in chapter three. Although most people clean a little at a time, I personally like to make an event out of it. We will discuss zone cleaning and tips for time constraints later in this chapter. For a major house cleaning - perhaps done once a month, once a year, or just before guests arrive, let's assume that time is not an issue. Make this process a meditation. Get out of your monkey mind for a little while and into your body by focusing all of your attention on the task of cleaning. Stay present in the moment and use your breath. With the right tools and a clear routine, you will feel empowered by making your home fresh and clean.

Get Prepared

- Put on comfy, preferably stretchy clothes
- Put on some energizing, uplifting or relaxing music depending on your mood
- Light a candle or some incense
- Grab a beverage to keep you hydrated

- Get everyone out of the house if possible because it's easier to do a deep clean without people in the way
- Open windows if possible
- Practice a few basic yoga postures to lubricate joints and prevent injury

Tools for Cleaning

Clean like the professionals. Complete the task in less time and in a more holistic way using the guidelines below for better results.

Extend Your Reach

Higher ceilings are not going away. Cleaning these areas can be a challenge. According to ISSA (International Sanitary Supply Association), cleaning with an extension handle is up to 10 times faster than cleaning with a hand held tool and a ladder. Not to mention safer. This applies to both hard-to-reach areas and regular floor cleaning, so the time savings can be huge. Think about professional painters and how they always put the paint roller on an extension handle. This is more ergonomic for the body, more efficient and can keep you from falling off a ladder.

Materials Matter

Modern cleaning tools include microfiber. If you haven't tried it and aren't using it, you should be. According to laboratory testing, microfiber picks up 99% of dust, dirt and bacteria that the naked eye can't see. Microfiber is truly amazing stuff! Its electrostatic properties grab dust, dirt and odor causing bacteria, trapping them in star shaped fibers until washed. These design features allow it to clean effectively without chemicals! Don't just push the dust around with traditional dusters - swap Ostrich feather, Lambs wool, and polyester dusters for microfiber and watch your cleaning time drop. Microfiber technology allows natural cleaning to be even more effective and can be machine-washed hundreds of times. Cleaning with reusable microfiber versus cotton, paper towels or disposable pads and cloths is more effective, more environmentally friendly over time and saves you money.

Use the Right Tool for the Job

I recently replaced an old vacuum cleaner with a new one that offers a system approach to cleaning and dusting. This one tool replaces the need for many. Having the best tools possible on hand can make all the difference in your cleaning routine. According to The Consumer Products Safety Commission in a 2012 report, each year there are more than 164,000 people treated in emergency rooms for injuries relating to ladders. Although a ladder, a cloth and an upside down umbrella is one way to clean a ceiling fan, it's probably not the fastest, safest or most efficient way to get the job done. Using cleaning tools that are designed for specific tasks like a lift away vacuum cleaner that allows you to easily grab cobwebs or a squeegee for windows is cleaning like the pros do it.

Extending your reach, using modern materials and specifically designed tools for the job, will help you have better results in a shorter period of time, without sacrificing safety.

Recommended Cleaning Items to Have on Hand

- Microfiber dusters that can be extended or attached to a telescopic pole if you have higher than nine foot ceilings
- Microfiber cleaning cloths
- A lightweight vacuum cleaner with various attachments that can help you clean floor surfaces as well as ceilings and corners nine feet or lower
- Microfiber flat mop for damp or dry mopping
- Scrub brush that is extendable or can be attached to a telescopic pole for better ergonomics
- Small hand held kitchen brush or tooth brush
- Lavender, lemon, orange, eucalyptus and sweet almond essential oils (a complete list is given in chapter seven)
- White vinegar
- Spray bottle

How to Clean

How to clean

1. Clean High & Dry

2. Clean Low & Then Wet

Clean High & Dry

This includes all dusting - ceilings, ceiling fans, bookshelves, railings and other surfaces. Do this first so that you can collect any dust and debris that has fallen down when you vacuum and mop. I do the hard-to-reach areas first using a telescopic pole with a microfiber duster or with my new vacuum cleaner and the wand attachment. I then target the lower surface areas by hand. Again, microfiber dusters are recommended for this task, as the fibers will collect the dust and trap it until washed instead of flinging it around the room and you won't need any chemicals.

Scented Dusting

Put a couple of drops of your favorite essential oil on your microfiber for the added aromatherapy benefit of scented dusting without the harsh chemicals of synthetic air fresheners. Lavender is great for bedrooms as it is relaxing and lemon is great for kitchens and living rooms as it is more invigorating.

Furniture Dusting

Put one cup of water and 15 drops of sweet almond oil along with 10 drops of lemon essential oil into the spray bottle. Spray mixture on a microfiber cloth and wipe down furniture (more on homemade natural cleaners in the next chapter). Move through the entire house completing the dusting and furniture polishing routine.

Clean Low & Then Wet

I recommend vacuuming and then damp mopping floor surfaces. I hardly ever sweep because a broom can just flick the dust and dirt around. A vacuum is a more effective way of getting pet hair and debris off the floor. Damp mop hard floor surfaces using the microfiber flat mop.

Damp Mopping

Put one cup of warm water, 30 drops of lemon essential oil and 2 tablespoons of white vinegar into the spray bottle. Spray mixture on sections of floor and then mop (double recipe for larger spaces).

Bathroom Surfaces

Use the same mixture as above with a microfiber cloth. Spray mixture on the cloth or directly on surfaces and wipe down. For scrubbing bathroom tile, shower doors and tubs, use a scrub brush. Spray surfaces with the cleaning mixture and scrub with the brush attached to handle or pole for speed and proper ergonomics. Move through the entire house completing the surface cleaning, vacuuming and mopping routine.

For hard water stains on glass shower doors, soak paper towels in vinegar and then spread them out and stick them to the glass door. Let then sit for 15 minutes and then come back and remove them. The water stains will have disappeared.

Sanitizing Cleaning Tools After the Job is Done

Put microfiber cloths, mop pads and dusters in the washing machine with rugs and bath mats using regular laundry detergent and then dry on low heat. Remove any large debris from mop pads by hand before washing. Clamp toilet bowl brush between the seat and the base with the brush over the bowl. Pour vinegar or bleach (if you must) over the brush.

Your entire home should be fresh, clean and best of all, chemical free! There are many things in life that you cannot control, but you can control how clean your home is and that is a very good thing!

Zone Cleaning

If time is an issue or you don't want to do a total house cleaning session, I recommend zone cleaning. This is the process of dividing your home into zones. The term *life hacking,* or simple ways to make life easier, can be applied here. One reality of increasingly busy lives is that for all but the most zealous housecleaners, cleaning tends to happen in brief bursts. These short bursts however tend to add up.

You will have to decide how you want to divide up the zones of your home based on how your house is laid out. In my house the kitchen, dining room, breakfast room and living room are next to each other so I consider this a zone. The master bedroom and bathroom is a second zone. The other bedrooms and bathroom are a third zone. And the downstairs area including the family room and entryway are the fourth zone.

This concept is extremely helpful when having children help with chores, for people who are time constrained or for those with a health concern. Select a zone to focus on and plan to spend 15 minutes in that area cleaning and straightening. Set a timer if necessary. Begin by straightening up the space and putting things back in their place. Then do whatever makes the most sense in the given time. Just making the bed in the bedroom or clearing the kitchen sink in the kitchen can make a big difference for example. Spending just 15-20 minutes in one zone may be enough for that day or week. If not, revisit it the following day and again each day that week until the zone is complete. It's that simple.

For more information on this and other useful tools like printable chore charts and detailed cleaning lists visit www.flylady.net or check out apps leveraged to help keep housecleaning on task and to make short bursts of cleaning more productive. Quite a few of these apps already exist such as Home Routines by Wunderbear ($4.99) or Chore Charts (free). In the next chapter I will provide lots of recipes for natural chemical free cleaners that are easy, safe and effective (and they smell good too).

How to Incorporate Yoga into Your Cleaning Routine

- Get prepared by dressing the part. Grab your music, meditation, beverage of choice and tools.
- Perform some basic stretches to loosen up muscles and avoid injury.
- Clean and clear your space with intention and presence for the greatest good of all concerned.
- Recite a mantra like OM or shanti (peace) or whatever you choose.
- Repeat an affirmation like: *I clean and clear this place. Only good is welcome here, this is sacred space.*
- Dedicate your act of cleaning to all beings or to someone in particular.
- See your cleaning practice as a form of karma yoga or selfless service.
- Practice bhakti yoga by cultivating a loving intention for yourself, your family and your home.

7 Recipes For Chemical-Free Cleaning

*Patchouli has always been a part of my
fragrance, like a line through my life.*
~ Julia Roberts

According to the EPA (Environmental Protection Agency), indoor air can be 10 to 100 times more polluted than outdoor air. This stat completely freaked me out when I saw it, but it makes sense. The main culprit is common household cleaners emitting toxic fumes. Household cleaners, often placed under the kitchen sink, release Volatile Organic Compounds (VOCs), when used and stored. These chemicals contain noxious toxins that are dangerous to adults, children, pets and the environment. If you have to wear rubber gloves to use these chemicals they are probably best avoided. Think about all of the household cleaners that we use without even pausing to consider that we are using them in a confined space with limited ventilation. Research shows that consumers express concern over health risks associated with cleaning ingredients. Nearly 6 in 10 agree that natural cleaning products are healthier than conventional ones. Your eyes, throat and hands don't need to burn to get the house clean.

Natural cleaners aren't really new. Vinegar has been used over time for a variety of cleaning tasks due to its high level of acidity. Most of our grandmothers knew about the wonders of vinegar. It is a natural, inexpensive disinfectant that can eliminate mold, bacteria, grease and germs. The smell can be a little astringent at first but once it dries, it fades away. You'll also be glad to know that it is environmentally friendly and very economical. I have discovered that if you have vinegar, you can clean just about anything. Add some essential oil for scent and anti-bacterial properties, and voila! You have natural cleaning. Visit the website www.vinegartips.com for 1001 uses for white distilled vinegar (and I'm not even kidding).

Essential oils also have been used throughout history for a variety of reasons. Our ancestors used herbs and essential oils to clean, disinfect and deodorize their homes. Essential oils are being used to make homemade household cleaners more often every day. The benefits to the environment and to the health of users make these homemade cleaners desirable. The cost of DIY cleaners is also much lower. Essential oils can be used to replace the chemicals in commercial cleaners. They can be used as disinfectants, air fresheners, grease cutters, antibacterial agents, anti-fungal agents, all purpose cleaners and whiteners. **Note of caution to pregnant women and diabetics:** essential oils can be dangerous because they are so concentrated. Pregnant women, diabetics and others with serious medical conditions should consult a doctor before handling any essential oils. Keep all essential oils out of the reach of children and pets. Some of the most effective types of oils are also the ones that smell the nicest. While not comprehensive by any means, here are the oils that are generally the most effective for cleaning.

- Eucalyptus works well as a grease cutter.
- Lavender is a sweet and woody scent that is an all purpose air freshener.
- Lemon or lemongrass make an effective all purpose cleaner and disinfectant as they have antibacterial and anti-fungal properties. They are also good for erasing odors.
- Jasmine is an effective all purpose cleaner and whitener as well as a mold and mildew killer.
- Thyme is one of the most effective disinfectants.
- Tea tree, cinnamon and clove essential oils are all very useful as cleaners and disinfectants as well.

All essential oils need to be diluted and mixed with other ingredients such as water, vinegar or carrier oils like olive oil to make an effective household cleaner. Armed with a few simple non-toxic and biodegradable ingredients, you can keep your home sparkling clean - naturally. Also, certain essential oils can stimulate lymphatic drainage or have antibacterial properties. Since it has many potential uses ranging from managing anxiety and nausea to helping with sleep, general relaxation, memory and attention, many individuals including cancer patients can benefit from aromatherapy via scented cleaning. According to the MD Anderson Cancer Center in Houston the benefits of aromatherapy are real.

For the natural cleaning recipes that follow, I have divided them for specific cleaning challenges room by room. I have also included the associated chakra for each space and how to bring it back to balance.

CLEANING SOLUTIONS

Ingredients

Dish washing soap
Sweet almond oil
Olive oil
Rubbing alcohol
Baking soda
White vinegar
Pure essential oils
Water

Equipment and Tools

Measuring cups and spoons
Spray bottles
Small kitchen scrub brush or toothbrush
Microfiber cloths

ROOM BY ROOM

BEDROOM

The Bedroom and the Sacral Chakra

Bedrooms can get musty and dusty and so can our sacral chakra. The sacrum or second chakra, located above the tailbone and below the naval controls our emotions, creativity and sexuality. This is the energy center that affects relationships and intimacy. If your bedroom needs attention, then the chances are good that your sacral chakra does too.

Rebalancing the Sacral Chakra and the Bedroom

After cleaning the bedroom, try some of these ideas to help rebalance your creativity energy center:

- Put freshly washed sheets on the bed
- Light a scented candle
- Add fresh flowers

Cleaning Challenges in the Bedroom

Often bedrooms contain carpets or rugs that need freshening and a good vacuum cleaning. Wood furniture also tends to get neglected and needs polishing.

Air-freshener

In just a few minutes using three simple ingredients, you can remove household odors and the spray also works well in the bathroom, on most fabrics, carpets and even in shoes.

The Recipe:

- 2 tablespoons rubbing alcohol
- 3/4 cup water
- 30 drops of essential oil (a few suggestions are jasmine, rose or lavender)

Put ingredients in a spray bottle, shake well and dial the nozzle to mist. This mixture will last for about a month.

Furniture Polish

If your wood furniture is in need of polishing, skip the commercial products and make your own.

Sweet Almond Polish

The Recipe:

- 1/2 cup sweet almond oil
- 30 drops of lemon essential oil

Put mixture in a spray bottle and shake well. Use with a microfiber cloth. This polish shouldn't be used on heavily waxed wood or wood with a polyurethane finish. These finishes often just need more waxing or wiping down.

Lemon Polish

The Recipe:

- 2 cups olive oil
- 30 drops of lemon essential oil

Put mixture in a spray bottle and shake well. Use with a microfiber cloth.

Carpet Cleaner

A lot can go wrong with carpet. Here are several options for getting it clean.

Spot Remover

The Recipe:

- 1 cup hot water
- 1 tablespoon dish soap
- Small kitchen brush or tooth brush
- Microfiber cloth

Put the dish soap into a bowl and then add the hot water. Dip the brush into the hot soapy water and working in circles, brush the stain until it is completely covered. Pat dry with the microfiber cloth.

Deodorizer/Freshener

The Recipe:

- 2 1/2 cups baking soda
- 30 drops eucalyptus essential oil
- 30 drops lavender essential oil

This quantity is enough for a 15 x 15 square foot room. Adjust recipe accordingly for larger or smaller rooms. Mix in a bowl or measuring cup, breaking up any clumps to disperse the essential oils. Sprinkle mixture on carpet and let sit for at least 15 minutes before vacuuming.

BATHROOM

The Bathroom and the Solar Plexus Chakra

Besides the kitchen, this room probably requires the most attention due to frequent use. This tends to be one of the least favorite places in the house to clean according to consumer research but one of the most important. The bathroom is the place where we eliminate and cleanse. The third chakra or solar plexus chakra, located in the center of the body between the naval and the rib cage controls digestion and elimination. This energy center also governs personal will and intention, physical energy and self-esteem. It is often in the morning during our bathroom routines that we set our intentions and prepare ourselves for the day ahead.

Rebalancing the Solar Plexus Chakra and the Bathroom

After cleaning the bathroom, try some of these ideas to help rebalance your power energy center:

- Use invigorating citrus scents
- Display a positive affirmation on your bathroom mirror
- Decorate with bright and invigorating colors

Cleaning Challenges in the Bathroom

Mold, soap scum, dirty grout and water spots on glass can make cleaning this space a challenge.

General Purpose Cleaner

The Recipe:

- 2 cups warm water
- 1/2 teaspoon liquid dishwashing soap
- 3 tablespoons white vinegar
- 30 drops lemon essential oil

Pour ingredients into a spray bottle. Shake well to mix.

Tile & Grout/Glass Cleaner

The Recipe:

- 1 cup water
- 1 cup white vinegar
- 10 drops lemon essential oil

Pour ingredients into a spray bottle. Shake well to mix. If this does not work for tile and grout, add baking soda to form a paste. Scrub with a brush in circles and rinse well. For glass use a microfiber cloth for streak-free cleaning.

KITCHEN

The Kitchen and the Heart Chakra

The kitchen is usually at the center of everything within a house. In fact, a house isn't really a home without a well stocked and smoothly functioning kitchen. This is where we prepare foods that nourish and sustain our bodies and where we come together with family and friends to eat, drink and be merry. Like the kitchen, the heart or fourth chakra is located at the center of our body in the chest. This center embodies love, laughter, joy and harmony. Just as the kitchen is the most important room in the house, the heart is the most important organ in the body.

Rebalancing the Heart Chakra and the Kitchen

After cleaning the kitchen, try some of these ideas to help rebalance your emotional energy center:

- Plan a dinner party for family and friends
- Put something green in the kitchen to help open the heart chakra
- Ask for help doing the dishes

Cleaning Challenges in the Kitchen

Funky smells from food prep? Marble surfaces? Stainless steel appliances? No problemo.

General Purpose Cleaner

The Recipe:

- 2 cups warm water
- 3 tablespoons white vinegar
- 30 drops Lemon essential oil

Pour ingredients into a spray bottle. Shake well to mix. Use with a microfiber cloth. I have found that this mixture will help control kitchen ants. They will avoid the acidic citrus in this cleaner and will stay off of counter tops and stoves.

Marble Cleaner

Marble, granite, and stone do NOT like having acidic (i.e.: citrus-based) cleaners used on them. Citrus or vinegar will actually cause "etching" on granite countertops. Not a good thing.

The Recipe:

- 2 cups warm water
- 3 drops liquid dishwashing soap
- 1/4 cup rubbing alcohol
- 10 drops sage essential oil

Pour ingredients into a spray bottle. Shake well to mix. Use with a microfiber cloth.

Stainless Steel Cleaner

The Recipe:

- 2 cups white vinegar
- 10 drops sage essential oil

Pour ingredients into a spray bottle. Shake well to mix. Use with a microfiber cloth.

Freshen Up the Stinky Garbage Disposal

Grind lemon rinds in the disposal to deodorize the sink or slice a lemon into quarters, slip them into the disposal, turn on the hot water and flip the power switch.

Put a Shine on Metal

Lemons are highly acidic, which enables them to cut through and loosen mineral deposits. Cut a lemon in half and sprinkle it with baking soda. Scrub brass and silver until shiny. Lemon is not quite strong enough for copper - use ketchup instead.

Clean up the Cutting Board

Kill bacteria and germs with the power of lemon. Cut a lemon in half and sprinkle it with Baking Soda. Scrub cutting board thoroughly and then rinse clean.

LIVING ROOM

The Living Room and the Throat Chakra

The living room like the fifth chakra or throat chakra is the center of communication. The throat focuses on expression, connection and speech. The living room tends to be the physical embodiment of the throat chakra. This is the room where family and friends come together to talk, read, enjoy movies and other form of entertainment or just relax.

Rebalancing the Throat Chakra and the Living Room

After decluttering and cleaning the living room, try some of these ideas to help rebalance your expression energy center:

- Cultivate some silence in your life and within the sacred space of your home for at least a few minutes everyday
- Scream into a pillow if you feel angry or frustrated
- Watch a funny movie or show and laugh out loud

Cleaning Challenges in the Living Room

Most living rooms offer dusting challenges of the hard-to-reach variety. Higher ceilings, ceiling fans, tall bookcases, ledges and windows can be hard to reach and even harder to clean.

Scented Dusting

Put a couple of drops of lemon, eucalyptus or jasmine essential oil on your microfiber duster. Let the oil dry for a few seconds and then begin dusting as usual.

Basic Glass & Window Cleaner

The Recipe:

- 1 cup white vinegar in a spray bottle

Use a microfiber cloth or squeegee for glass surfaces and windows. Add a telescopic pole to the squeegee as needed for hard-to-reach windows.

HOW TO CLEAN YOUR YOGA MAT

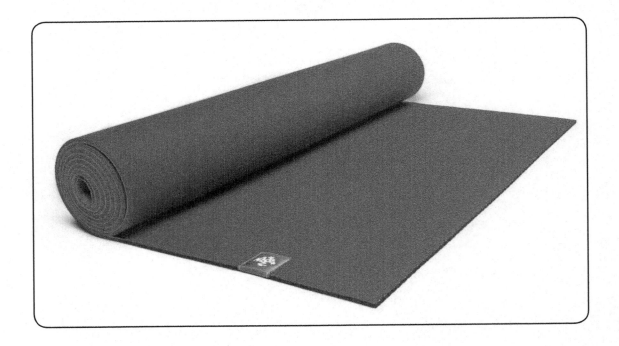

The Recipe:

- 1 cup warm water
- 3 tablespoons white vinegar
- 15 drops of essential oils like eucalyptus, lemongrass, lavender, mint, or tea tree

Pour the ingredients into a spray bottle. Spray your yoga mat cleaner liberally over the surface of your mat. If your mat seems especially dirty, let the cleanser sit and soak in a bit before cleaning it off. Wipe the yoga mat with a microfiber cloth. Now repeat on the other side. Allow your mat to air dry, which should take only about 5 to 10 minutes. If it takes longer than this, try rubbing your mat down more with a dry microfiber cloth to remove the excess water and speed up the drying time.

NOTES

8 A Spiritual Spring Clean

*I look forward to spring cleaning and putting things in their place.
It's therapeutic for me.*
~ Kimora Lee Simmons

Have you ever noticed the energy in a yoga class, church or temple? There is a non-physical spaciousness to these places. These are places that are constantly being blessed with sound, candles, incense, music, mantra and prayer. The result is a sacred space that feels safe, peaceful and deeply nurturing. Why not practice energy clearing in your own personal space? Many people perform energy cleansing and space dedication rituals for new homes and businesses. This is a fabulous way to remove negative and stale energy that may be lingering from past illnesses, arguments or upsets. It's all about clearing out the old and making way for the new. No experience needed - only intention and an open mind. It is preferable to do this when no one else is home. I recommend doing it 3-4 times a year and more heavily in the spring when you can open windows and doors. This should be done after regular decluttering and cleaning has taken place.

Tools for Energy Cleansing

Ancient cultures have used sound and elements from nature to perform space-cleansing rituals. Choose at least one from each category below to use in your cleansing practice.

Sound

You can use bells, Tibetan singing bowls, music, chimes or drums. I generally use a simple meditation chime. You can find such items at most new age stores or online. Of course, sound can also include your own voice chanting. The sound of OM has a very powerful effect on the energy in any room.

Scent

You can use sage, sandalwood incense or candles of various scents. I like to use a sage spray as it's safer, smoke-less and lasts longer.

Nature

You can use flowers, plants, crystals, stones, feathers or even seashells from your last trip to the beach.

Create a Temporary or Permanent Special Space Called an Altar

Altars are intended to act as a catalyst for shifting thoughts and energy from a lower vibration reality to the higher vibrations of the spiritual realm. There is no specific blueprint for constructing an altar. I have several altars in my home and one on my desk at work to help balance out unseen electromagnetic energy created by computers, cell phones and wireless frequencies that can affect your physiology.

Select a space to place your altar. I usually start my cleaning and clearing rituals in the bedroom where I spend most of my time at home. Set up your altar there or any place in your home that you feel is appropriate to begin and end the ritual.

Give the altar boundaries to symbolize a separation between the everyday and the spiritual. It encourages the mental shift from one attitude to the other when you physically cross that boundary and enter the altar area. Place items on your altar from the list above. Dedicate your altar space to cleaning, clearing and purifying the energy in your home and in your life. I use a short prayer like the following:

May all lower level or negative energy be transmuted to its highest possible
good and may any energy that cannot be transmuted
go some place where it can be loved.

The intention here is that you aren't sweeping your bad energy down the street to your neighbor's house. Instead, you are actually transforming the energy in your space.

Image of bedroom altar

Image of home office altar

Image of work office altar

Now that your altar is ready, you will be walking around the inside of your home - moving along each wall of each room and spending longer in certain spots where you feel the energy is a little heavier or stuck. Begin and finish at the altar you have set up. Be as present and in your body as you can. Stay hydrated, remember to breathe and above all trust your intuition. Stop and rest whenever you need to, particularly if your mind starts to wander. Mindful awareness is the key.

Open a window or door if possible. Light your incense or sage, grab your holy water, diluted essential oil or room spray. Play soothing music in the background if you like while you work. Start in one corner of the room and work from bottom to top. I use a mantra like: *I clean and clear this place, only good is welcome here, this is sacred space.* If you are using incense or sage, let the smoke waft up and down the walls and into the corners. If you are using a spray, you will spray high and low every few feet. As I work my way around each wall, paying extra special attention to corners and the centers of the rooms throughout the house, I repeat my mantra dozens and dozens of times. Before I leave each room I sound the meditation chime to finish off the energy clearing and further purify the space.

How To Perform a Spiritual Spring Clean

- Start by clearing as much clutter as you can and perform your basic cleaning routine.
- Only perform an energy cleansing ritual when your energies are strong and your thoughts are clear. This can be done alone or with others who hold similar intentions.
- Pay close attention to the corners – they can hold stuck, dead or heavy energy.

I trust that you will notice a change and a difference in the way your home feels once you have cleansed and blessed the energy in your space.

9 Create A Custom Space With Ayurveda

*A house is not a home unless it contains food
and fire for the mind as well as the body.*
~ Benjamin Franklin

Ayurveda is a roughly 3,000 year old system of natural healing that originated in the Vedic culture of India. Although suppressed during the years of foreign occupation, ayurveda has been enjoying a major resurgence in both its native land and throughout the world and is the oldest continuously practiced health-care system around. Tibetan medicine and traditional Chinese medicine both have their roots in ayurveda. Early Greek medicine also embraced many concepts originally described in the classical ayurvedic medical texts dating back thousands of years.

More than a mere system of treating illness, ayurveda is a science of life (*Ayur* = life, *Veda* = science or knowledge). It offers a body of wisdom designed to help people stay vital while realizing their full human potential. Providing guidelines on ideal daily and seasonal routines, diet, behavior and the proper use of our senses, ayurveda reminds us that health is the balanced and dynamic integration of our environment, body, mind and spirit. Ayurveda is built around the five elements of ether, air, fire, water and earth, which constitute what we refer to as doshas.

These doshic constitutions, known as prakruti, are determined at the moment of conception, according to ayurveda. Once you understand your personal doshas by taking the quiz below, you can begin to find out why you react to certain situations, colors, scents, and flavors. Then you will have the knowledge of how to bring yourself back into balance by designing your environment to best suit your needs.

It is my goal here to focus predominately on the overall well-being in the surrounding environment of the home. Ayurveda is a very large subject that extends to diet, herbs, supplements, health and beauty treatments as well as daily routines. While I will give some general dietary guidelines by dosha type, I will not go into great detail. If you would like to explore this subject more in depth I would recommend the following books:

Yoga & Ayurveda Self-Healing and Self-Realization by Dr. David Frawley
Perfect Health The Complete Mind/Body Guide by Dr. Deepak Chopra
The Chopra Center Cookbook: A Nutritional Guide to Renewal
/ Nourishing Body and Soul by Dr. Deepak Chopra

My prakruti is pitta (fire) and kapha (earth). My pitta and kapha scores are only about two digits apart, so this makes me bi-doshic. Some people have almost equal amounts of all three, but that is more rare. The majority of people will have one or two predominate doshas. Although I love the hot summer months, my pitta nature tends to get out of balance and I can end up with odd skin rashes and a tendency to feel cranky and overheated if I spend too much time outdoors. I know not to even think about taking a hot yoga class or a hot bath during the summer months and I do most of my cleaning routine in the morning before it gets too hot out. I tend to perform my yoga practice in the late afternoon after the sun has gone down. I have the opposite problem during the winter. My kapha nature tends to get out of balance and I feel sluggish and lethargic. I have to be conscious about getting enough exercise and eating the right foods. Lighting, colors and scents play a big role in keeping me energized and balanced during the cold and dreary indoor months.

Take the Following Dosha Quiz to Determine Your Mind/Body Constitution

This quiz gathers information about your basic nature - the way you were as a child or the basic patterns that have been true most of your life. If you developed an illness in childhood or as an adult, think of how things were for you before that illness. If more than one quality is applicable in each characteristic, choose the one that applies the most. For fairly objective physical traits, your choice will usually be obvious. For mental traits and behaviors, which are more subjective, you should answer according to how you have felt and acted most of your life. Rate each description for each subset with a 5 for the description which is most like you, a 3 for the description that seems second most like you and a 1 for the description that seems least like you. Rate each description and then total the columns.

Dosha Quiz

Frame	I am thin, lanky, and slender build	I have a medium, symmetrical build	I have a large, round or stocky build
	◯	◯	◯
Weight	Low, I often forget to eat	Moderate, it is easy for me to gain or lose weight	Heavy, I gain weight easily and have difficulty loosing it
	◯	◯	◯
Eyes	My eyes are small and active	I have a penetrating gaze	I have large pleasant eyes
	◯	◯	◯
Complexion	My skin is dry, rough or thin	My skin is warm, reddish in color and prone to irritation	My skin is thick, moist and smooth
	◯	◯	◯

Dosha Quiz

Hair	My hair is dry, brittle or frizzy	My hair is fine with a tendency towards early graying or thinning	I have abundant, thick and oily hair
	⬭	⬭	⬭
Joints	My joints are thin and prominent and have a tendency to crack	My joints are loose and flexible	My joints are large, well knit and padded
	⬭	⬭	⬭
Sleep Pattern	I am a light sleeper with a tendency to awaken easily	I am a moderately sound sleeper, usually needing less than eight hours to feel rested	I sleep deeply. I tend to awaken slowly in the morning
	⬭	⬭	⬭
Body Temp	My hands and feet are usually cold and I prefer warm environments	I am usually warm, regardless of the season and prefer cooler environments	I am adaptable to most temperatures but do not like cold, wet days
	⬭	⬭	⬭

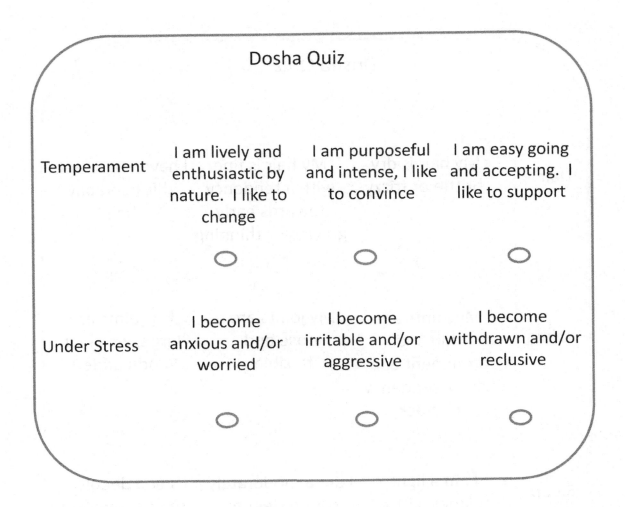

Dosha Quiz

Temperament	I am lively and enthusiastic by nature. I like to change	I am purposeful and intense, I like to convince	I am easy going and accepting. I like to support
	○	○	○
Under Stress	I become anxious and/or worried	I become irritable and/or aggressive	I become withdrawn and/or reclusive
	○	○	○

The column that received the highest number is the dosha principle that is the most predominant force in your overall mind body make-up. The column that received the next highest number is the secondary force in your constitution. The lowest scoring column while still an active force in your mind body physiology, is the least dominant in your particular energy field. If your numbers total highest in the first column, you have a predominance of vata or air in your mind/body constitution. If the numbers are highest in the second column, you have a predominance of pitta or fire in your mind/body. And if the numbers total the highest in the third column, you have more kapha or earth. Most of us have one or two doshas, which are most lively in our nature, with the remaining one(s) less significant. Consider the following information based on the results of your quiz.

For additional information on the Dosha Quiz visit – www.doshaquiz.chopra.com

Doshas

According to ayurveda, each of us inherits a unique mix of three mind/body principles, which creates our specific mental and physical characteristics. These three principles are called *doshas*. The three doshas are known as **Vata, Pitta,** and **Kapha.**

If we are predominantly **vata** or air, we tend to be thin, light and quick in our thoughts and actions. Change is a constant part of our lives. When vata is balanced, we are creative, enthusiastic and cheerful. But if vata becomes excessive we may develop anxiety, insomnia or irregular digestion.

If the **pitta** or fire dosha is most lively in our nature, we tend to be muscular, smart and determined. If balanced, we are warm, intelligent and good leaders. If out of balance, pitta can make us critical, irritable and aggressive.

If we have mostly **kapha** or earth in our nature, we tend to be stable, have a heavier frame and think and move in a more leisurely way. When balanced, it creates calmness, sweetness and loyalty. When excessive, kapha can cause weight gain, congestion and resistance to healthy change.

Using the principles of ayurveda, we can identify our mind/body nature and use this understanding to make the most nourishing choices in our lives. It is common for people to have a blend of characteristics and usually one will tend to be dominant. The information below will help you bring your dosha(s) back to balance naturally and then we will discuss how to use this knowledge to create a more harmonious environment at home.

Vata Dosha

When vata is out of balance, too much air has accumulated in the mind, body and environment. The result is a sense of ungroundedness. The best way to balance excess vata is to bring more earth and stability into the physiology. Think relaxing and grounding. Balance vata through touch and sound. That's why massage is so often used in ayurveda. Vata is a dosha that quickly goes out of balance and can quickly come back into balance. A good hug from a loved one or friend can bring the out-of-sorts vata person back to center. A warm oil massage will balance and calm vata almost instantly, whether you do it yourself or go to a massage therapist. Vatas are also very sensitive to sound, after all, there's not much in the ears except air and space, which is what vata is made of! Lots of vatas live in the ears, so if the wrong radio station or TV program is on, vatas will feel very uncomfortable and distracted quite easily. Some vata imbalances related to touch and sound include: constipation, insomnia, joint pain, anxiety, depression, worry, mood swings, lack of concentration, ringing in the ears, headaches and general aches and pains.

Balancing Practices for Vata

- Go to bed and awaken at the same time every day.
- Meditate twice a day to quiet the mind.
- Practice yoga to connect with your body.
- Wear relaxing fragrances.
- Eat three meals per day and favor sweet, sour, and salty tastes.
- Perform a slow daily self massage with warm relaxing herbalized oil.
- Drink herbal tea.
- Look for opportunities to create rhythm and routine in your life.
- Diffuse relaxing fragrances into your environment with candles and incense.
- Finish things once you start them.

Pitta Dosha

When pitta is out of balance, too much fire has accumulated in the mind, body and environment. The result is a sense of internal and external combustion. The best way to balance excess pitta is to bring more space and coolness into the physiology. Think soothing. Balance pitta through sight therapy. Whether that's cleaning up a cluttered house, a messy desk or a disorganized closet, pittas love to organize. They will feel a little out of control if what they see is a mess and they will quickly look to start cleaning it up. This need for organization and cleanliness is because pittas are very sensitive and occasionally critical. Some pitta imbalances related to sight include: red or itchy eyes, tension headaches, insomnia, pink eye, dizziness or lightheadedness and irritability.

Balancing Practices for Pitta

- Spend time outside and in nature as often as possible.
- Favor cooling tastes - sweet, bitter and astringent.
- Meditate twice a day to soothe the mind and relax the body.

- Schedule some space or quiet time in your day.
- Perform a slow self-massage with herbalized oil.
- Wear soothing fragrances.
- Favor cool, soft colors - blue, green and white.
- Drink herbal tea.
- Diffuse soothing fragrances into your environment.
- Try to be more playful.
- Engage in non-competitive physical activities like yoga.
- Eat with full awareness.
- Stay cool.

Kapha Dosha

When kapha is out of balance, too much earth has accumulated in the mind, body and environment. The result is a sense of sluggishness, congestion and dullness. The best way to balance excess kapha is to bring more movement and circulation into the physiology. Think invigoration. Balance kapha through the senses of taste and smell. Kaphas love to eat! They love to make foods, taste foods and serve foods. The combination of a kitchen that smells divine and food that tastes even better is irresistible to a kapha. Some kapha imbalances related to taste and smell include: weight gain, lethargy, cloudiness of mind, greed, excess attachment, low self worth, depression and high cholesterol.

Balancing Practices for Kapha

- Awaken at sunrise.
- Look for opportunities to create healthy change.
- Favor pungent, bitter and astringent tastes.
- Avoid eating when you're not hungry.
- Be spontaneous and try new things.
- Wear invigorating fragrances.
- Clean out your space.
- Drink invigorating herbal tea.
- Diffuse invigorating fragrances into your environment.
- Favor bright strong colors - reds, oranges, and yellows.
- Meditate twice a day to get clear on your intentions and desires.

- Perform a vigorous self-massage with warm invigorating herbalized oil.
- Exercise daily!

How to Choose Colors That Create Balance in Your Life

When it comes time to paint your walls step number one is finding a product that won't emit harmful chemicals in your home. That means paints with the lowest possible emissions of volatile organic compounds, or VOCs. Then comes the hard part or the fun part depending on your attitude - choosing the right color. Should it be light or dark? Hot or cool? Stimulating or calming? By working with your emotions, the color of a room can subtly affect your sense of well-being and in the long run maybe even your health.

Color therapy, also known as chromotherapy, is the principle that certain colors are infused with healing powers. The seven colors of the rainbow improve balance and healing in the mind and body. This form of therapy also works in conjunction with hydrotherapy (water) and aromatherapy (scent) to enhance the healing effect. For example, vatas may benefit from earthy colors, pittas can balance their natural tendencies with cooling, soothing colors and kaphas may want to choose bold, mobilizing colors. Color plays a significant role in how people respond to time spent in a particular space. For example, the coloring of walls and fabrics for a space affect a person's response to that room. Often, this response to color directly correlates with a person's comfort and well-being. Chromotherapy research shows that color can actually help heal the body.

The Code of Color

- Red raises blood temperature and stimulates circulation. Red is used to care for people with anemia, fatigue, paralysis and exhaustion.
- Blue is soothing. It is used for cases of inflammatory conditions, burns, and bruises. It also helps with eczema, psoriasis, rashes and sores. In addition, blue

helps alleviate tension, stress and problems with the immune system. It is believed to relieve insomnia, anxiety, high blood pressure, migraines and skin irritation.

- Yellow is used to aid in digestion and liver function. Yellow is thought to have decongestant and antibacterial properties that act as a cleanser for the body. It has been known to help relieve rheumatism and arthritis.
- Green creates balance and harmony within the body. It is especially good for heart and blood problems. It is known to influence the human cell structure and muscles.
- Orange gives vitality to the body and is associated with the kidneys, urinary tract, and reproductive organs.
- Purple is associated with the eyes, ears, nose and mouth. It helps with head congestion and sinuses and is known to calm the nervous system.

At times color therapy has been known to generate an overwhelming emotional response in individuals. It is important to refrain from overdoing spaces with too much color. Whether color is used to encourage healing or to enhance use of a space, color therapy can be exceptionally powerful.

Dosha Color Recommendation

Vata

Balancing colors for vatas are warm or calming. Yellows and golds are very pleasing in vata decor. So are white, violet, blue and deep reds. Avoid bright red - it's far too stimulating.

Pitta

Because pittas tend to be hot, they need a cooling environment to stay in balance. Stick with soft, pastel colors to soothe away tensions. Blues and greens are particularly beneficial, as are pinks and roses.

Kapha

Kapha needs the stimulation of bright, hot colors. Pick up the energy level with reds and oranges.

THE AT-A-GLANCE COLOR CHART

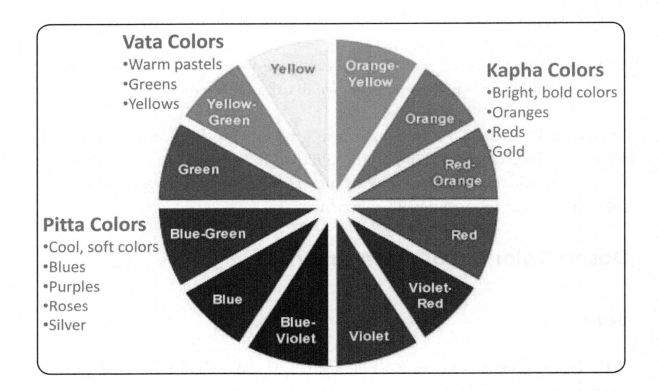

Vata Colors
•Warm pastels
•Greens
•Yellows

Kapha Colors
•Bright, bold colors
•Oranges
•Reds
•Gold

Pitta Colors
•Cool, soft colors
•Blues
•Purples
•Roses
•Silver

The Power of Scent

Never underestimate the sense of smell. Odor has the quickest and easiest pathway to the brain. That's why many ayurvedic practitioners believe that inhaling certain aromas can balance one's dosha, reduce stress and promote overall healing. Here are the scents that are right for your dosha.

Vata

- Flower scents like rose and geranium
- Sweet citrus scents

Pitta

- Sweet, bitter, or astringent scents. Try chamomile, lily, honeysuckle, iris, or jasmine

Kapha

- Pungent, stimulating scents such as eucalyptus, cedar, pine and sage
- Peppermint

Yoga and Ayurveda

Yes, ayurveda and your dosha will also have an effect on your yoga practice. In fact, most ayurvedic scholars agree that you really cannot practice one without the other. People with different doshic constitutions take class together all of the time, but students with ayurvedic knowledge can adapt a class to their personal needs through attitude, intention and breath-work. Vatas should practice slowly and deliberately. Kaphas need to challenge themselves more and pittas need to relax and avoid overheating.

Personally, I am pitta with almost as much kapha. Every time I try a hot yoga class I come away feeling overheated and agitated; yet I need to move, so a vinyasa class is a good option. Use your dosha as a guide to help you find the style of yoga that is right for you.

Ayurveda and Food

The following chart published by the Chopra Center as part of their *Perfect Health Program* is a general guide. For my own diet, I avoid dairy and beans when possible even though ayurveda finds these foods to be satvic or pure. Any food allergies or dietary constraints should also be taken into consideration. You will also notice that meat is not listed here as ayurveda recommends avoiding animal protein. Use your best judgment and listen to your own body's wisdom when making decisions about diet.

	TO PACIFY VATA	TO PACIFY PITTA	TO PACIFY KAPHA
Basic Qualities	Favor: warm, oily, heavy foods, sweet, sour and salty tastes	Favor: cool foods and liquids, sweet, bitter and astringent tastes	Favor: light, dry, warm foods, pungent, butter and astringent tastes
Dairy	Favor: warm, oily, heavy foods, sweet, sour and salty tastes	Favor: warm, oily, heavy foods, sweet, sour and salty tastes	Favor: warm, oily, heavy foods, sweet, sour and salty tastes
Fruits	Favor: avocados, bananas, cherries, mangos Reduce: apples, pears, cranberries	Favor: grapes, melons, cherries, apples, ripe oranges Reduce: grapefruits, sour berries	Favor: apples, pears Reduce: bananas, avocados, coconuts, melons
Vegetables	Favor: asparagus, beets, carrots Reduce: sprouts, cabbage	Favor: asparagus, cucumbers, potatoes, broccoli, green beans Reduce: tomatoes, peppers, onions	Favor: all vegetables except tomatoes, cucumbers, sweet potatoes
Beans	Favor: mung, dahl and tofu Reduce: all others	Favor: all beans except lentils	Favor: all beans except tofu and soybeans
Grains	Favor: rice and wheat Reduce: barley, corn, millet, buckwheat, rye and oats	Favor: rice, wheat, barley, oats Reduce: corn, millet, brown rice	Favor: barley, corn, millet, buckwheat, rye and oats Reduce: rice and wheat
Spices	Favor: cardamom, cumin, ginger, cinnamon, salt, nutmeg, asafetida	Favor: coriander, cumin, fennel, sugar Reduce: hot spices like ginger, pepper, mustard seed	Favor: all spices

How to Practice Ayurveda in Your Home

Tap into the science of life designed to help you stay vital, while realizing your full human potential. Ayurveda reminds us that health is the balanced and dynamic integration between our environment, body, mind and spirit.

- Take the dosha quiz to determine your unique mind/body constitution.
- Choose colors that are right for your home based on your dosha.
- Choose fragrances that help to balance you out and soothe your senses.
- Practice yoga postures that are suited to your type.
- Eat foods that create balance.

10 Space Plan With Vastu

*Chaos is inherent in all compounded
things. Strive on with diligence.*
~ Buddha

Vastu, the ancient science of design and architecture, originated during the Vedic civilization, which many scholars assert flourished as early as 6000 years ago in India and other parts of South Asia. Vastu is arguably the world's oldest holistic design system and the precursor of feng shui. These ancient concepts are the roots of the modern-day holistic living movement. Vastu shows us how to create interior spaces that honor the rhythms of the universe and re-establish harmony with nature and ourselves.

Although vastu is not commonly known or practiced in the US, I became interested in this subject and did quite a bit of research when I began writing this book. There is a lot of information on Kathleen Cox's website www.vastuliving.com and in her book, *Vastu Living*. This is a vast subject, and I will not go into every detail, but I will share enough of the basics here to get you started with a more modern and Western approach to this ancient and Eastern technology. Traditional texts on this subject are designed for building a space from the ground up so that the structure faces the correct direction and so that all of the rooms are arranged according to the ideal vastu blue print. This will apply to very few of us, but don't throw the baby out with the bath water here. By having just 51% correct vastu you can help shift the energy in your space and make a big difference in your well-being. You, your family and your guests will feel a positive difference.

Vastu, the science of architecture and design, is a Sanskrit word that means *dwelling* or *site*. While the practice of vastu applies to buildings and interior design, the word vastu also applies to the human body. Vedic scholars recognized that the human body is an example of vastu. Vastu, yoga and ayurveda share the same spiritual philosophy and goal, to increase our well-being and inner balance so that we can free our minds of distracting thoughts and turn inward to connect with the soul. While yoga and ayurveda focus primarily on the body, vastu focuses on the personal environment in which we spend most of our time - our home. By following the principles of vastu, we create environments that are harmonious and calming. In these environments, we aim to shut out the world and create sanctuary for ourselves and for our families. To put Vedic philosophy into practice, vastu asks us to do our best to adhere to three critical principles. We must:

- Honor the five basic elements
- Respect nature in all of its forms
- Celebrate our self and our special identity

By adhering to these basic principles we are reminded that all of creation is divine. When you let these three principles guide your decisions in the arrangement of your furnishings, you set in motion rhythms that move from corner to corner and room to room.

Basic Element Grids

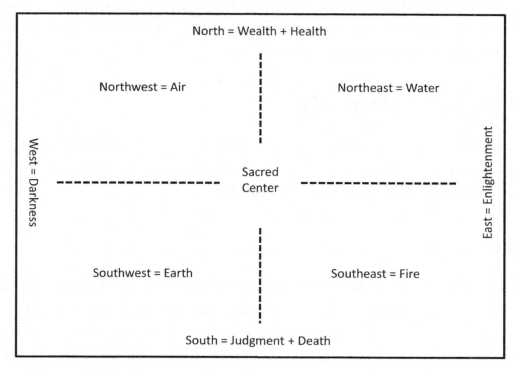

Location of the Five Basic Elements in the Northern Hemisphere

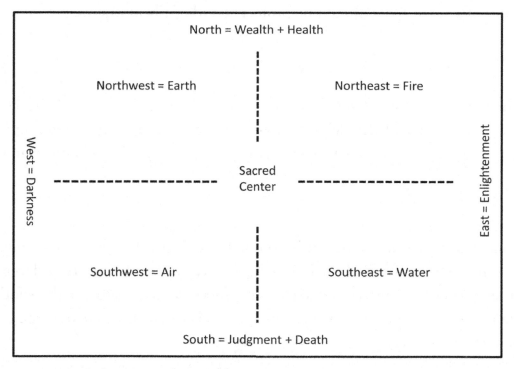

Location of the Five Basic Elements in the Southern Hemisphere

Note: The principles that follow are based on living in the Northern Hemisphere and readers in the Southern Hemisphere should convert the directions using the Southern Hemisphere chart above, which shows the effect of the earth's rotation below the equator on the practice of vastu.

The Five Basic Elements

In the practice of vastu, each element has a predetermined location within the land, the structure and within each room. The following is a description of the basic elements and the guidelines for space planning.

Space

The center of every room in your home is dedicated to the element of space or ether. This is what we refer to as the sacred center. Spiritual energies collect here and disperse in the form of positive vibrations that shower everyone in the space with good emotions. Space or ether is essential in creation. In vastu, this center area of each room is compared to the womb, which houses the embryo and the navel, which is considered the center of your body. The womb and the navel are fragile, so the center of a vastu space should be protected and not bear any weight.

Air

The northwest quadrant belongs to air. Air represents prana or life force. Air represents movement. If the element of air is allowed to move freely through your space, quick thoughts and bursts of creativity that inspire healthy change can occur.

Fire

The element of fire resides in the southeast quadrant. Warmth, passion and emotional intensity are characteristics of the fire element. Ideally, your barbecue grill, outdoor generator or any equipment associated with fire should be kept in the southeast quadrant of your property. It would also be ideal if your kitchen were located in the southeast quadrant.

Water

The northeast belongs to the element of water. Water is calming, soothing and reflective. This quadrant is referred to in Vedic texts as the gateway to the gods. This portion of your property and/or room should be left open and unblocked. A pool or pond in this quadrant of your property is even more ideal. Tall, heavy furniture should not be placed in the northeast quadrant where it can block out the spiritual power and cosmic energy. This portion of each room is also referred to as the zone of tranquility.

Earth

The earth element is in the southwest quadrant. The strong and heavy properties connected to the element of earth serve as a healthy and protective barrier. Tall and heavy furniture is typically recommended for this location.

The assigned location of the five basic elements encourages the placement of delicate and lightweight furnishings in the north and the east, bulky, tall furnishings in the south and the west, and a protected sacred center, which remains uncovered and unburdened by weight.

Bringing the Outdoors In

Vastu asks us to show our respect for nature by bringing it into our home. The presence of nature comforts us and helps us to relax - lowering cortisol or stress hormone levels and boosting the immune system. Plants also help detox the air and remove impurities from our environment. My husband and I have plants throughout our home, wherever they can thrive. Once they get going they really don't need a lot of attention and they greatly enrich our lives and impact the energy in our home for the better making it worth the effort.

Breakfast Room

Family Room / Home Office

Family Room / Home Office

Dining Room

Living Room

Using your dosha (mind/body constitution) identified in the previous chapter on ayurveda, consider the placement of furniture in your space. Is the placement of furniture in your home aggravating your dosha? Do you have heavy pieces of furniture in the northeast? Are you covering your sacred center? Are you bringing nature into your space? The following example using my bedroom, illustrates the layout of furniture and the challenges associated with this room.

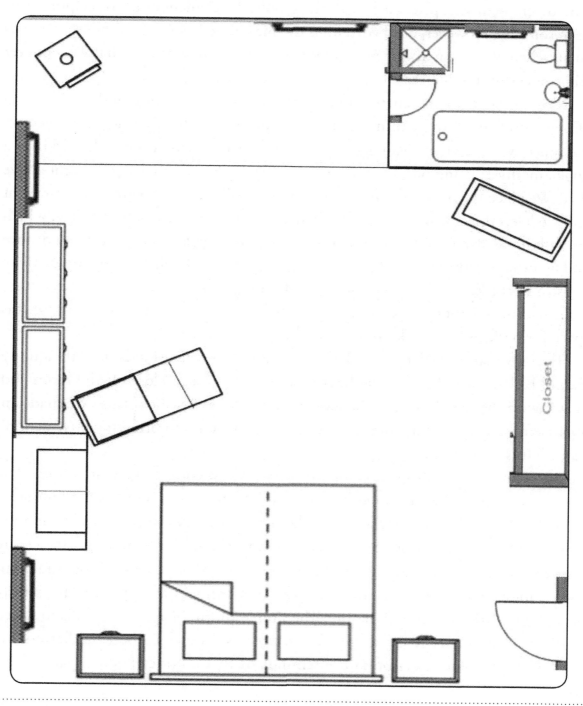

My bedroom is located in the northwest quadrant of the house, which is not ideal because the northwest is the element of air. My husband and I are predominately pitta dosha, which carries an abundance of fire and the element of air aggravates this quality. My husband also has a secondary dosha of vata, which is air, so this quadrant leaves him feeling restless at night. Even our large family room downstairs in the southwest quadrant of the house would be a more ideal location for us than our current bedroom placement with the grounding element of Earth helping us to sleep soundly. However, our bedroom *is* the master bedroom in the house, and has an attached bathroom and plenty of light, so it is highly unlikely that we will ever relocate within the house.

Making do with the current quadrant that we are working with, we look to placement of furniture within the space to optimize vastu. By placing the bed on the south wall we take advantage of as much earth element as possible. We have a huge amethyst sitting on a shelf directly above the bed and a large skylight above that. We place the heaver furniture on the west wall because it can bear the weight and we keep the east wall relatively open except for our closet and the TV, which we will discuss later on. In the north, we have a sliding glass door and a wood stove and no other furniture so that positive energies can flow freely into the space. There is also a serene koi pool just outside of the sliding glass door that lets us enjoy nature from within our room. The sacred center is left free and open. We often use this space for performing gentle stretches and yoga postures.

The only major problem is the TV. It is located right where our zone of tranquility should be. But we like it in the bedroom because we can close off the room and heat it with the wood stove in the winter. What do we do about this? We made an appeasement with several large crystals on the TV stand to bring in an element of nature. It is a work in progress.

So, seeing that every space cannot be 100% vastu correct, make it at least 51% correct. You may discover some similar conflicts in your home that defy physical solutions. What do you do when a problem in your home seems unfixable in your practice of vastu? You restore harmony through the use of appeasements. When a space is not vastu correct, it can have an impact on your well-being and your constitution. If we can't fix it, we can make an offering or an appeasement to help bring it into balance through nature. The simplest form of appeasement is to select an object from the world of nature -plants, crystals, seashells, wood and flowers are good examples. An object of nature reminds us that all of creation is part of the supreme creative life force. When you surround yourself with these items that are reminders of your divinity, they serve as a powerful antidote to the disharmony that creates trouble in your space. Natural objects in your home act as balancing agents to help restore wellbeing. Your appeasement affirms your belief that harmony must prevail in your home and within your own physical form. It is important that the items that you choose for your home have a positive effect on you, whatever they may be.

How To Practice Vastu

- Remember that everyday, you are reacting to your surrounding environment.
- Avoid clutter.
- Don't put furniture against the wall if possible - 4 inches away is recommended.
- Circular or square? Use circular furniture if you want movement or animation and use square furniture if you want to relax or be still. Example: the breakfast table should be round to invoke energy while the dining table should be square or rectangular to elicit calm.
- Use the designated location grids for your hemisphere.
- Honor the nature elements in furniture placement.
- Make appeasements to the elements using nature when your space won't allow you to follow vastu.

11 7 Essential Steps to The Yoga of Cleaning

The most courageous act is still to think for yourself. Aloud.
~ Coco Chanel

Too many of us live in a state of chronic stress where lifesaving mechanisms attached to fight or flight syndrome never shut down. Too much of this over a prolonged period of time and good health can be threatened. Consider these 2013 stats from The American Psychological Association - stress has an impact on the personal and professional life of 48% of all American adults and at least 77% say that they regularly experience physical symptoms caused by stress. The majority of us attribute stress to the conflicting demands of work, home and social pressures. We all struggle to meet the demands of our jobs and personal lives and we usually sacrifice our own needs in the process. The frequently overlooked factor is that the home itself can be a source of discomfort, rather than the sanctuary that it should be. When you enter your home, you should be able to find a place to sit in serenity. You should feel welcomed and nourished by your personal environment. Your home should be a source of harmony. So often however, we live in a space and never claim it as our own. The rooms inside are just places where we happen to live and spend a lot of time. This attitude has broad implications that affect our well-being. Your home is not living up to its fullest potential if you don't view it as an extension of yourself.

Practicing the yoga of cleaning in your life means caring for your body as you care for your home and caring for your home as you care for your body. It's that simple. But, if we're going someplace new, it's good to have a roadmap. So here it is – 7 steps to the yoga of cleaning! The essential guide in a nutshell. Here we go...

1. Conscious Movement

Studies have shown yoga to be beneficial for both physical and mental health. Just start moving. A little at a time if necessary, and as time permits. Remember, that just 20 minutes a day of vigorous housework can cut stress by as much as 20%. When it comes to yoga, being in a class is great, but most people only go to class once or twice a week. I recommend learning a basic set of yoga postures that you can practice on your own every day or before you perform your cleaning routine. Yoga does not need to be complicated to be effective. It only needs to be performed consciously.

Breakdown of Benefits

- Improved flexibility - roughly 35% increase in flexibility after 8 weeks of practice
- Oxygen to the brain
- Increased lung capacity
- Peace of mind and slower breathing = less stress
- Increased arm, leg and back strength
- Improved physical and emotional well-being
- Increased libido
- Better posture
- Increases metabolism

Because yoga is so very important to your overall well-being, I would like to offer you a bonus chair yoga sequence that you can do anywhere, even at the office.

Chair Yoga Postures

Overhead Stretch

- Raise your right arm slowly over your head, gently stretching at the shoulder.
- As you fully extend your arm, feel the stretch along your side.
- As you lower your right arm, raise your left arm over your head, stretching at the shoulder.
- Alternate one arm and then the other, breathing easily with each extension.
- Repeat three to five times per side.

Forward Fold

- With your hands over your head, slowly bend forward from the waist.
- Gradually bring your hands to the floor next to your feet.
- Let your head relax between your knees.
- Rest your abdomen on your thighs and breathe slowly and deeply, allowing your breath to massage your organs.
- After a few breaths, slowly come up one vertebra at a time.

Side Twists

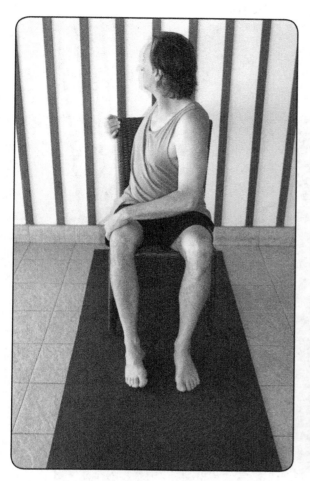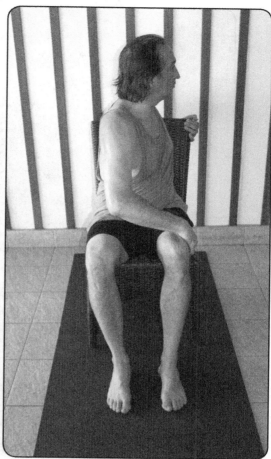

- Cross your right leg over your left thigh.
- Place your left hand on your right thigh.
- Reach behind you with your right hand and grasp the chair, using it to rotate your spine to the right.
- Keep your head aligned with your spine and remember to breathe.
- Hold for a couple of breaths.
- Release, and repeat on the other side.

The Arch

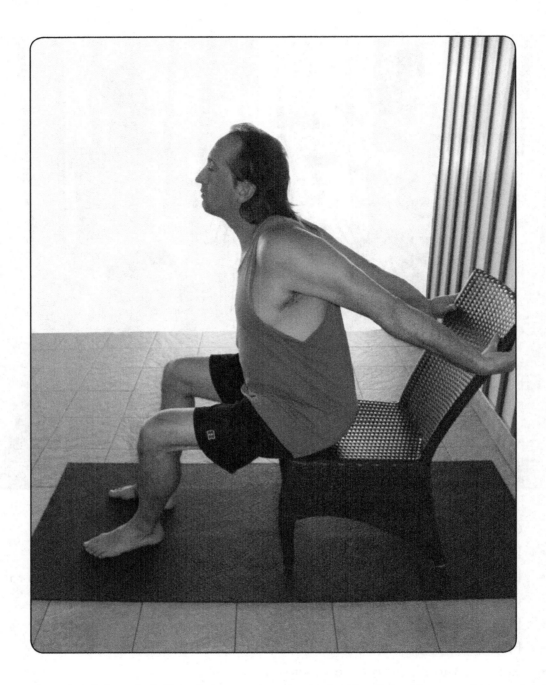

- Place both hands behind you, grasping the back of the chair with your hands.
- Inhale slowly and deeply, lifting your chest up toward the ceiling.
- Extend your neck and stretch from the lower back.
- Hold for two breaths and then relax.
- Repeat three times.

Knee Stretch

 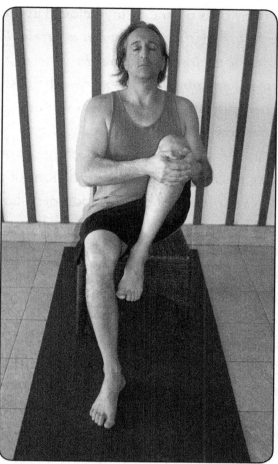

- Grasp below your right knee with both hands.
- On your exhalation, pull your knee up to your chest, feeling the stretch in the hip and thigh.
- Drop the shoulders back and down, lift the chin and pull the knee closer into the chest.
- Hold for several breath cycles and then repeat on the opposite side.

2. Conscious Breathing

In the words of one of my beloved and dearly departed teachers Dr. David Simon, *the first thing that we do when we arrive on this planet is inhale. The last thing that we do when we leave is exhale. In between we respire about a half billion times, usually without any conscious attention.* The best anti-stress medicine we have may be right under our noses. Obviously, everyone alive knows how to breathe but few people know how to breathe correctly. We are taught to suck in our guts and puff out our chests. As a result, we have become a world full of shallow chest breathers primarily using the middle and upper portions of our lungs. Only yogis, singers, athletes and doctors are aware that the abdomen should expand during inhalation.

If you watch babies or small children breathe you will see the belly go up and down, deep and slow, as they naturally practice pranayama. With age though, most people shift from natural abdominal breathing to a much more shallow style of chest breathing. This is one of the main advantages of yoga - it reminds us how to breathe literally and figuratively. Breathing awareness alone can have remarkable results such as lowered blood pressure, improved digestion, decreased anxiety, improved sleep and energy levels. I have seen the difference that conscious breathing has on my students and many of them share that they sleep better after a yoga class where they practice proper breathing techniques. Old habits are hard to break and we often return to unconscious patterns. When we are willing to explore the unseen layers of our bodies, we can tap into the immense creative power that lives at our source. Follow the guidelines below and perform conscious breathing on a regular basis to stay healthy, stress-free and calm.

- After performing any of the three breathing exercises in chapter four, take a moment to notice how your mind and body feel afterward. Use the belly breath if you are feeling stressed or anxious. Use the rhythmatic breath if you are feeling depleted and tired and need to cultivate more energy. And use the alternate nostril breath if you are feeling pain, tension, tightness or constriction.
- Try using breath instead of any other support system that you would normally utilize. Instead of taking an aspirin for a mild headache, try alternate nostril breathing. Instead of going for another cup of coffee, try rhythmatic breathing. Instead of getting lost in the moment and saying something that you will regret later, try belly breathing. You will be pleasantly surprised at how effective this can be. Use your breath to enliven your body's natural healing capabilities.

3. Declutter Your Space

Decluttering can cause an energetic upheaval. You may uncover objects that trigger memories - some good, some bad. Nevertheless, clearing clutter is one of the best ways to boost your energy, get yourself out of a rut, improve your health, remove obstacles and create space for the new to arrive. Clearing clutter is a proven therapy for creating change in your life. *Now* is always the perfect time for a focused clutter clearing session.

Once you have cleared the old and unwanted from your space and your life you can begin to make room for something new. If you have a goal that affects your entire space, try doing something small in each room to prepare for that new reality. For example, if you want a new love in your life, create room in your closet. Planning on expanding your family? It may be time to repaint that spare bedroom. You will find that all areas of your life will flow more easily after you have put your home in order. Your newly organize home will become a sacred space for you to enjoy. Follow these basic tips to get started.

- Start small. Pick a room, a closet or just a drawer and get started sorting it out.
- Commit to clean. Spend 10-15 minutes a day straightening or decluttering a room or the house. This will pay off over time.
- Go for the gusto. Put on the pressure by hosting a dinner party or inviting the in-laws over for the weekend.

4. Clean Naturally

Start by eliminating one toxin at a time. Take a look at the products that you use on a regular basis and consider how they affect your environment. Are you contributing to the toxicity of your home? Many of us use the products that our mothers used without much thought because we tend to trust the brands we know. Both new technologies like steam cleaners and old basics like vinegar or baking soda make for powerful cleaning combinations that bridge the old and the new.

Consider how you clean your home. Are you using the best and most effective cleaning tools in the best and most effective way possible? Are you working harder than you need to? Do you see cleaning as an opportunity to extend your well-being and refresh the energy in your home? Love it or hate it, we all have the opportunity to make cleaning more enjoyable and more effective. The following tips will help you clean like a pro.

- Clean high to low, and then dry to wet for better efficiency.
- Use microfiber instead of cotton or paper towels whenever possible for performance.
- Use natural cleaning solutions and keep your home toxin free while getting the aromatherapy benefits of essential oils.
- Use telescopic tools to extend your reach in hard-to-clean areas for better results in a shorter period of time, without sacrificing safety.

5. Spiritualize Your Cleaning Routine

Spiritual housecleaning goes beyond the dirt and clutter to address the underlying negative energy that can create unseen problems in your home. As with anything else in life, you can make this as simple or as complicated as you like. Spiritual spring clean anytime to clear negative and stale energy that lingers in your home using intention. You can conduct a special ritual using candles, sage or incense or just create an intention while performing basic cleaning tasks. Clean, clear, bless, honor and protect your home and loved ones using the methods of choice. Whether or not you perform a spiritual housecleaning in your weekly routine, it is a good idea to give your entire home a thorough energetic cleaning at least once a year. I like to do mine in the spring, both because this is the traditional time of year to do a major house clean and because after a long cold New England winter it is nice to open the windows and let in some fresh air. Depending on where you live and your life circumstances, you may decide to do your yearly spiritual housecleaning at a different time - say in September when your kids are back in school or on your birthday to prepare for the year ahead or on New Year's Day. Whenever you choose to do it, here are some simple spiritual spring cleaning tips. Feel free to use all of these or alter them to fit your needs.

- Start by opening some windows or at least one window at the top of the house.
- Gather whatever tools you plan to use - mundane or magical.
- Set your intention for cleaning, clearing, protection and blessings.
- Use sound, scent and nature to help elevate the energy level in your home.
- Create an altar space to honor your home and all of the things that you love.

6. Create a Custom Sacred Space with Ayurveda

What's your dosha baby? Ayurveda explains the nature of everything in the universe. It is a compelling way of looking at life. Ayurveda "types" people according to physical features and personality traits. It tells us how we tick and how we relate to the rest of the world. Using your dosha, you can create the most ideal space for your special mind/body constitution. With this invaluable information, your home will nourish, soothe and support you rather than irritating you and causing you additional stress.

Two pittas in a pod - my husband and I are both primarily pitta dosha. Our secondary doshas are on opposite ends of the spectrum. This means that we need to decorate with cool, soft colors to keep our fire in check. Blues, greens and silvers are particularly good. We have a small koi pond right outside of our bedroom window so that we can hear the sound of water during warmer months. We are happiest in the temperate northeast climate and tend to keep the fridge stocked with veggies and salad-makings. Knowing our natural tendencies and how to keep our home and ourselves in balance is such a blessing. Once you have your dosha(s) down, follow these basics to keep your home balanced.

- Use the at-a-glance color chart for your dosha and select colors that will bring you back into balance naturally.
- Incorporate fragrances into your space that soothe your senses.
- Enjoy sounds that bring you back into harmony.
- Design your diet with your dosha in mind.
- Practice yoga poses that keep you in balance.

7. Space Plan with Vastu

Although quite different in many ways, vastu and feng shui share some common core timeless design approaches. Remember that vastu, when translated means *the environment* and that everyday you are reacting to your surroundings. By following vastu as much as possible, we honor the rhythms that control the universe and establish harmony with nature and ourselves. For the decorating-phobics among you here is a basic overview for creating a more positive and streamlined space.

- Clutter and order cannot co-exist. Decluttering the home helps us clear out the old, stale, stagnant, and unwanted so that we can make space for new things, new creations and new energy.

- Colors impact mood. Combine ayurvedic dosha balancing colors or simply select colors that convey the range of human emotion. Pinks and oranges trigger joy while greens and blues create calm. Reds inspire passion while black and white combinations embody grace. Surround yourself with colors that please you and positive energy will flow undisturbed within your abode.
- Lighting is everything. The choice of lighting can set the tone for a room. Bright lighting can be welcoming or energizing - awakening the mind to the possibilities that lie ahead. Lower lighting can trigger relaxation at the end of the day, be seductive or calming. Let lighting set the mood for your space.
- Bring nature indoors. Whatever your style, plant life and natural elements form a connection to the great outdoors. The more high tech your life may be, the more you need Mother Nature.

Claim your space! It is my goal that *The Yoga of Cleaning* will help you take the power of well-being into your own hands. Decluttering, cleaning with natural ingredients and energy clearing with intention help us to spiritualize our entire cleaning routine and create sacred space.

Yoga, when practiced, unites the mind, body and spirit. Combined with it's sister philosophies of ayurveda and vastu, we have a powerful system for creating health, nourishment and healing at home. Putting together this entire system of ancient wisdom and modern tools, we have a tremendous resource that can transform our environment and us if we apply it in our daily lives. I wish you peace and happiness along the way.

Namaste

Glossary

Ahimsa - Non-violence

Altar - Sacred space for personal or meaningful or natural objects

Aparigraha - Generosity

Asana - Third branch of yoga, seat or position, pose

Asteya - Honesty

Ayurveda - The Indian system of alternative medicine

Brahmacharya - Appropriate sexual control

Chakra - Energy wheel or center

Dharana - Sixth branch of yoga, mastery of attention and intention

Dharma - One's true purpose in life

Dhyana - Seventh branch of yoga, witnessing awareness

Dosha - Mind/body constitution made up of earth elements

Ishwara-Pranidhana - Surrender to the divine

Kapha - Earth dosha

Mantra - Sound or word that is repeated. Sometimes there is a meaning, and sometimes just a vibration

Meditation - Bringing awareness inward and quieting the mind

Namaste - The divine light in me honors the divine light in you

Niyamas - The second branch of yoga, rules of personal behavior

OM - A vibrational universal sound that is said to have been the sound of creation

Pitta - Fire dosha

Pranayama - Fourth branch of yoga, breathing exercises

Pratyahara - Fifth branch of yoga, directing the senses inward to become aware of the subtle senses

Samadhi - Eighth branch of yoga, state of being settled in pure unbounded awareness

Sanskrit - Ancient Vedic sacred language

Santosha - Contentment

Satya - Truthful speech

Shanti - Peace

Shoucha - Purity

Sutra - Stitch or thread

Svadhyana - Spiritual exploration

Vastu - The Indian system of space planning that predates feng shui

Vata - Air dosha

Vedas - A large body of texts originating in ancient India

Yamas - The first branch of yoga, rules of social behavior

Yoga - Union or yoking of the mind, body and spirit

Sources of Additional Information

Yoga

The Seven Spiritual Laws of Yoga by Deepak Chopra, M.D. and David Simon, M.D., John Wiley & Sons, Inc., 2004.

The Yoga Sutras of Patanjali, Translated and Introduced by Alistair Shearer, Bell Tower, 1982.

The Yoga Bible by Christina Brown, Godsfield Press Ltd., 2003.

Chakras

The Seven Spiritual Laws of Yoga by Deepak Chopra, M.D. and David Simon, M.D., John Wiley & Sons, Inc., 2004.

The Chakra Bible by Patricia Mercier, Octopus Publishing Group, 2007.

True Balance by Sonia Choquette, PH.D., Three Rivers Press, 2000

Ayurveda

Vital Energy by David Simon, M.D., John Wiley & Sons, Inc., 2000.

Perfect Health The Complete Mind Body Guide by Deepak Chopra, M.D., Three Rivers Press, 1991,2000.

Yoga & Ayurveda Self-Healing and Self-Realization by David Frawley, Lotus Press, 1999.

Vastu

Vastu Living: Creating a Home for the Soul by Kathleen M. Cox, Da Capo Press, 2000.

Vastu: Transcendental Home Design in Harmony with Nature by Sherri Silverman, Gibbs Smith, 2007.

The Author

Jen Carter Avgerinos is a creative and passionate writer and marketer of products, brands and technologies that help people to live more fulfilled lives. She has worked in consumer packaged cleaning tools for the last 7 years and for many years in the fashion industry prior to that.

Jen is a certified yoga teacher and has been teaching in Connecticut for the last three years. She studied hatha yoga and *The Seven Spiritual Laws of Yoga* at The Chopra Center in Carlsbad, CA. Jen is also a certified prenatal/postnatal and kids yoga teacher. She has taught hundreds of classes and workshops and publishes a blog on her website www.adore-yoga.com. She lives in Connecticut with her husband Paul.

CPSIA information can be obtained at www.ICGtesting.com
Printed in the USA
LVOW03s1612280715

447956LV00001B/25/P

9 781452 592701